To Jane:

Celebrate the gift!

Letters to Our Daughters

MOTHERS' WORDS OF LOVE

KRISTINE VAN RADEN

AND

MOLLY DAVIS

BEYOND
WORDS
Publishing
I N C

Beyond Words Publishing, Inc.
28027 NW Cornell Road, Suite 500
Hillsboro, Oregon 97124-6074
503-531-8700
1-800-284-9673

Editor: Sue Mann
Design and composition: Rohani Design, Edmonds, Washington
Cover photo: David Van Raden
Production: Nancy Deahl
Proofreader: Marvin Moore

Printed in the United States of America
Distributed to the book trade by Publishers Group West

Library of Congress Cataloging-in-Publication Data

Letters to our daughters : mothers' words of love / [edited by] Kristine Van Raden &
    Molly Davis
        p. cm.
     Includes index.
     ISBN 1-885223-50-1
     1. Mothers and daughters—Correspondence. I. Van Raden, Kristine. II. Davis,
Molly, 1953– .
    HQ755.86.L47 1997
    306.874'3—dc21   96-39990
                                                          CIP

The corporate mission of Beyond Words Publishing, Inc.: *Inspire to Integrity*

To my wonderful mom and best friend; to my daughters, Sarah and Katie; to Todd and Ally; and to David, the love of my life.

K. V. R.

To my mother, whom I treasure; to my precious daughters, Haley and Lauren, and my stepdaughters, Clare and Valerie. Tom, I thank you from the bottom of my heart for my studio. I love you.

M. D.

We both express our sincere thanks and appreciation to all who made this book possible. For those of you who opened your hearts to us and shared such genuine love, we thank you.

CONTENTS

Introduction   5

INTRODUCTION

"SHE HAS HER father's eyes. I think she has her mother's smile." But most certainly she has a daughter's path to follow. Not unlike the millions of daughters who have come before her, she will have to negotiate for herself the challenges that lie ahead. And above all others, the person she will look to as her role model will be her mother.

As human beings we all share in life's trials and tribulations. We must make choices every day that move us forward, set us back, or hold us steadfast to the status quo. If we could see ahead, we would probably tend to take the path of least resistance. No one welcomes those situations that seem to test the stuff we're made of. Although it is true that those lessons do strengthen our character, there are times when the challenges seem too great.

No sooner does it seem that we as young adults have waged tough battles and managed to survive than we find ourselves caretakers and protectors of infants more important to us than anything we ever dreamed possible. As we look into their faces we may recall our journeys, which started with no more fear and trepidation than what our babies now feel. Yet, the journeys that lie ahead are awesome, and like any journey, ripe with the possibility of failures and triumphs, joys and pain.

The transformation that occurs from daughter to mother is one that all women who choose to have children have in common. Not that their paths are any less diverse than their unique lives, but there is a mutual understanding that draws together women who recognize the depth of the challenge, the responsibility, and the potential for a relationship unlike any other.

Letters to Our Daughters began almost fifteen years ago, although we (Kristine and Molly) were unaware of it at the time. That was the beginning of our lives as mothers. Throughout the years we have shared many things. The greatest of these, however, is the love and passion we have for our children. We have often marveled at the unconditional love we feel for our daughters, with a depth and intensity different from any we have experienced. We began to wonder what other mothers would say about their feelings for their daughters. And so it was that one cold and rainy morning at the Oregon coast the idea for *Letters* was born. We began to envision a book that would celebrate the relationship between mother and daughter. It was a thought that sprang forth on its own, presenting itself as an idea whose time had come, a gift ready to be shared by mothers and daughters everywhere.

We had often talked about how important it would be to write a letter to each of our daughters, expressing our love and sharing our dreams and hopes for her, a keepsake that she could treasure and reflect on in years to come. It seemed that a collection of letters from mothers to daughters would be an intimate way to share this celebration with the world.

Our first task was to decide on the issues that face mothers and daughters today. Then we had to find women who would be willing to write letters and share them publicly. Friends and acquaintances gave us names; our lists soon included women throughout the United States and around the world. We used the yellow pages, newspaper and magazine articles, anything we could think of to contact women for this project. We stopped people on the street and in the checkout line at the grocery store. We felt that we could even dial a wrong number and find out that it really wasn't a wrong number at all but rather a connection to yet another woman who wanted to write a letter for the book. One phone call would lead to another; one contact would lead to ten more.

When we began, we didn't know about the journey that lay ahead and the women we would be privileged to meet along the way. We began to connect with people and communities we might not normally touch in our everyday lives. But we quickly realized that we were not strangers; we stood on the common ground of love. Many women asked us, "Why did you choose me? I am nobody special." The truth we were able to tell them and the truth shared in this book is that each person is significant and has something to offer that no one else can. It is evidence that amidst the ordinary one finds the most miraculous and extraordinary.

We were awed and humbled by the letters written and shared at our request, the wisdom we witnessed, and the love we received. We were allowed access to the intimate places of these mothers' hearts, and our lives were transformed by their words. We will never be the same because of this experience, and for that we are deeply grateful. When it became apparent that this book was a gift to us, we realized it was our responsibility to care for and honor that gift so others might share in its blessing.

The diversity of the letter writers provided us with a tapestry rich in texture, complex in color and detail. Yet through it all runs a common thread that binds women one to another regardless of their circumstances, education, belief system, culture, work, or age: what they desire for their daughters is a future filled with hope, the strength and courage to meet the challenges, and above all else, a deep belief in their unique value.

We invite you to immerse yourself in the wisdom these mothers so graciously shared. Laugh with them and cry with them. Hold your breath as their daughters step forth on their own, and hold these mothers in your arms as you experience their pain, tenderness, and joy.

There is much in the world that seeks to divide us. It is our hope that this book will unite and inspire all who read it.

Letters to Our Daughters

DEAR JANICE,

I welcome this opportunity to express my love for you because I feel so fortunate to be your mother. As I write this letter, my thoughts go back to your childhood, recalling so many nostalgic and irreplaceable memories. You were a happy, generous, vivacious, and loving child, and those years flew by so fast for me.

Soon you were an adult and I discovered that I not only had a daughter, but I also had a friend.

BETTY SHARES BOTH HER PRIDE IN HER DAUGHTER AND THE LOVE AND HAPPINESS POSSIBLE IN THEIR RELATIONSHIP.

I hope one of my gifts to you has been my ability to "let go," so that you could find your own path in life. I feel my role in your life is to encourage you to seek your dreams so that you can experience all the wonderful life-enriching adventures life can hold for you. A parent's love can be like the "wind in your sails," helping you to open wide, wide in belief, as wide as a sail. I want to encourage you to do the things in life that are important to you. I want you to live life to the fullest and be able to look back on your life with few regrets and lots of fond and rewarding memories.

You must understand that there is within all of us the power that will give us the answers we seek. Janice, you have proven that you have that power and have come out on top. You have trusted you and with this confidence have found happiness. With this happiness you have been able to pass it on to others that you love. I am so proud of you!

I LOVE YOU DEARLY,

MOM

DEAR DARLENE,

*T*his is a hard letter to write. My heart aches to know you are going through what I went through many years ago. Divorce is more common now than it was in 1928, but I know that doesn't make it less painful. I thought your long marriage was rock solid. This is such a shock. I guess none of us ever knows what lies ahead.

I worry about what you are going to do. Will you stay in your house? Will you sell real estate again? What are your plans?

Since I don't have my own home to offer you, I could come and be with you if you need me. I want to help.

MATILDA, A DIVORCED NEBRASKA FARMWIFE WHO RAISED HER THREE CHILDREN ALONE, WRITES UPON LEARNING OF HER DAUGHTER'S DIVORCE.

When your father left I felt so alone and afraid. I was grateful that my father made a home for us on his farm. I had a large garden, raised chickens, and sold eggs. We managed to get by. But times are different now. Life is not as simple.

You are blessed with three wonderful children, and if I was to give you any advice it would be this: be strong, never lose your pride, and continue to trust in God. You will have times, as I did, when you will wonder if you can survive the pain. You will. Never forget that.

I send you my love. My prayers are with you always.

MOTHER

My Beloved Daughter,

I come into your room at night to kiss you and cover you with a blanket, just like when you were little. You are a big girl now, but to me it is like before when you were my little baby. We lived in Siberia for two years before you were born. I had much difficulty with you. You were born early and were very sick. You gave me many difficult times because you didn't sleep and didn't eat. When you were only one month old I took you back to Odessa. Back to the sunshine and warmth of the Black Sea.

Your father and I did not like what was happening in Russia. The people of Russia are very good, but not so much the government. The ideas behind communism were good but did not work. Even very educated people in Russia couldn't get higher paying jobs. We felt that this USA is utopia. We thought that we all would be happier here.

SVETLANA, A RUSSIAN IMMIGRANT, WORRIES ABOUT THE CULTURAL DIFFERENCES BETWEEN HER COUNTRY AND AMERICA AND PONDERS THE EFFECT THE NEW ENVIRONMENT WILL HAVE ON HER TEENAGE DAUGHTER.

We have been in America now for eight years. You were just a young girl of eight when we left Russia. Now you are a beautiful young woman who is trying to find her own way. I must tell you that there are times when I am afraid for you, afraid for your future. This country is so different than the country I was raised in, and sometimes I don't understand what you are going through here.

When I was a young girl in Russia my family was not poor, but we worked hard for what we had. I was very close to my mother and two younger sisters. My mother was older when she had children. She was practical and not always easy for my sisters to talk to. I often took care of them, and they would talk to me about life. I was the one who talked with Mama and told her everything. My mother was someone who I respected very much, and I always loved when she told us stories. Fairy tales were my mama's stories. She knew so much.

In my family and in Russia education was so important. My parents encouraged us to learn. My mama was always my first teacher, but as I grew up I learned from many teachers: Shakespeare, for example. I didn't just read books, I became absorbed in them. I learned about and understood about so many different people. The characters in the books became my teachers. When I married I had my own small library in my apartment. I read and read.

It has not been easy for you and I in America. I am almost 50 now. I must work very hard to care for my children. I don't make much money, but I am responsible and I am providing for you. I see you struggle, also. You are a Russian girl with a Russian family, but you long to be American. I don't think you are getting a good education. You do not read. We often fight. I try to teach you things that are important, but you do not respect me or what I have to offer you. But I believe that you are a good girl, and I think that this is normal teenager and that someday you will listen.

When we lived in Russia, I made your older sister study English all the time. The other children would be playing, but she would have to carry her books and go to lessons. She used to say, "I hate you, I hate you." Now she lives in New York. She has a good job and a fine husband in medicine. Now she says, "Thank you for making me study." Someday you will thank me and respect what I have tried to teach you.

Anna, there is much I want for you. I want to teach you how to be a woman. I remember when I was 13½ years old, a very popular boy at school admired me. I was not as beautiful as other girls, nor did I have beautiful clothes like other girls. But he wanted a friendship with only me. I loved him and he loved me. We never even kissed, but just looked at each other. I have such sweet memories.

I have never thought of myself as very beautiful, and yet men have always been drawn to me. So, I asked myself, why me? I have an answer for you, my daughter! I am a feminine woman. I have a heart that is clean and I take pride in my appearance. I respect myself, I am educated, and I am strong. I want you to give yourself these same things. I remind myself of what my mama said to me. She said that every woman must be like iron inside. I didn't understand this for so long. Now I understand that she meant a woman must be strong, know her own power, and be able to handle anything, because life is not easy.

I want you to be able to talk to me and feel that I can be a help to you. I still talk to my mama. I look up in the sky and I tell her about me, about my kids, about everything. I feel very close to her. I can hear her say, "Don't cry, I'll never leave you. I will always be with you."

I LOVE YOU,

MAMA

A I S H A *("Life" in Swahili),*

Now it is time to write the serious things of my heart, things which I have longed to tell you from our beginning of time. I talk to you as a mother, a sister, and your number one girlfriend. I am proud of you for all the things that you are. I wish I could physically be with you on your journey of life; I know you'll be phenomenal. Your God-given gifts, girl, are yours alone. It's your obligation and responsibility to use these God-given gifts to find your purpose and remain on that narrow road to life.

You've been well taught by two people who've been around, from gangsters to the elite.

KARLA SPEAKS OF THE IMPORTANCE OF LEARNING TO LOVE, PURSUING ONE'S DREAMS, AND UNDERSTANDING CULTURAL UNIQUENESS.

This makes you unique. You will be influenced by others as well. Young women today have opportunities that I wanted to achieve, but circumstances didn't permit it. I was born literally in the cold and have struggled for my life, my identity, for who I am and what I'm about deep in my soul. You must deal with so many of the same issues: prejudice, sex, racism, education, the battle of the sexes, and money. So always remember life is about choices.

You have the dream of becoming a surgeon. You've worked hard in school. You've set high expectations for yourself. I will work day and night to see that your education is my utmost priority for as long as it takes to achieve your goal.

Education is so vital in today's society. Without it you can live and die at the same level you started, broke. So many of our people have given up on life, escaping to drugs, alcohol, crime, racism, teenage pregnancy, and divorce, eventually being robbed of their hope for a future.

Hopelessness breaks down cultural connections. Let me elaborate. You see, from the beginning of time, in Africa, we were a people of distinguished character, with great prosperity, education, and fine arts. Torn from our roots, deprogrammed, then reprogrammed, we were shipped to America. We were beat or beat to death, forced into family separation with language barriers and unable to communicate with one another, to slave as beasts in the fields. I am thankful to our ancestors for surviving through it all, doing what was necessary to preserve what is true. You have another intricate part of your heritage—that being of Native American descent. In order for us to survive, from the time of the white man's first landing in America native Indians saw the white man's way, saw the destruction, devastation, and had compassion for the Negro slave. Thus the Indians took us in, hid and protected us from bounty hunters, fed, clothed, and cared for us.

I've always taught you to be independent, think for yourself, plan and provide for yourself. You can't lose if you go to high school, buy your own car, go to medical school, and then purchase your own home. When you're ready to marry, find a qualified man who satisfies your emotional needs. Then, together you can decide about children. Keep your options open! A good education and a good salary will help you to do that.

I've always believed that it is up to each one of us to teach each other about diversity. Diversity is not just about color, race, or creed, but racists, also, who will never change and eventually have to answer to whom? Almighty God, Himself. So always ask yourself, What is the outcome of negative treatment? remembering you could be in those shoes. Then choose to do the right thing listening to your inner self (that third eye).

It saddens me to see today's generation believing they can start their lives like their parents and grandparents before them, believing they can get by in life with little or no education, with addictions and an attitude of being "dead in the head."

Your willingness to get involved in other people's lives and always giving will allow you your rewards. We, as women, rarely give ourselves time to rest and renew our strength. So, in the process of caring for others, always take care of yourself, sometimes first.

Aisha, we have a bond that I believe could never be broken. It began at the time of conception and cemented over the years. We celebrate our lives together, our heritage of the past, and the future that is ahead. I am so proud of all you are and will be. I hope you continue to work towards *your* dreams and aspirations. Always continue to ask for any assistance you might need, and talk to me about anything. Remember, Jehovah God is your first strand and He does provide.

LOVE ALWAYS,

MAMA

DEAR DEBBIE,

*T*oday is my anniversary. I was reminiscing this morning and recalling that painful morning on February 5, 1981, when I called you from work to tell you I had to go to the hospital. Your concern was, what kind of a physical illness did I have? However, I was calling for a far different reason.

I shall never forget the cry from you and the frightened concern in your voice. "Please, Mother, what is the matter with you?" As I replied, I trembled, so frightened and ashamed. My words came out hesitating and unsure of myself. "Debbie, they say I have a problem . . . an alcohol problem. I am an alcoholic." These words were the most shameful and difficult thing I had ever said to you. I could hear on the other end of the line your sharp intake of breath and your inability to reply. I immediately said, "Please don't cry, please don't be ashamed that I am an alcoholic." After a long pause you

JULIA, A RECOVERING ALCOHOLIC, CELEBRATES HER SOBRIETY WITH THE HELP DEBBIE HAS GIVEN HER.

whispered, "Oh Mom, I am not crying because you are an alcoholic or because I am ashamed of you, but because my prayers have finally been answered." It was then that we shared our tears of joy and relief.

During the early part of my recovery, I had to make amends to people I had harmed by my actions and words during my alcoholism. It was so difficult to tell you and your brother how sorry I was for all the

14

wrong and pain I had caused you. Yet it became a feeling of peace within me to put to rest the guilt of my past behavior.

Deb, I will always be grateful to you for allowing me to express my grief and shame of self-indulgence. As I poured out words of remorse, you sat there with a soft and peaceful smile, listening to me, accepting me with your love. I said, "I am so sorry for being a terrible mother and for having failed you in so many ways." With unfathomable forgiveness you replied, "You were never a terrible mother, nor have you ever failed as one. My brother and I just lost you for 10 years. . . . Now you are back."

So today, because of your understanding, I celebrate my return to sobriety. This letter is to thank you for being the joy of my life and the living proof of my wellness.

YOUR LOVING MOTHER,

JULIA

DEAR RACHELLE,

*W*hen you were just three months old, your father left our family to be with another woman. Although we have talked about it, and you realize that he loves you very much, times were tough. We had to go on welfare, and that was very hard. I still remember riding the bus to the welfare office and being told I might have to wait all day to be able to see a social worker, so we waited—all day!

That day, the light at the end of a very long tunnel appeared. The social worker told me that the system provided temporary help for families like ours. *Temporary* meant that it would not always be this way. But for the next two and a half years, we lived on very little. We received $476 a month and free cheese, cereal, and juice, along with $189 in food stamps we collected at the post office each month. Not very much for a family of four. It was so difficult living without enough money or a car. You went without nice clothes and fancy toys. We ate a lot of macaroni. I went to college on a federal grant. I was determined to provide a good future for all of us. I want you to know that the thought of that better future for you kept me going.

LARAMIE REMEMBERS THE HARD TIMES SHE AND HER DAUGHTER HAD WHILE THEY WERE ON WELFARE AND ASKS HER DAUGHTER TO REMEMBER THE LESSONS LEARNED DURING THOSE YEARS.

Two and a half years later we reached the light at the end of our tunnel. I called the welfare office and told them that they would not be seeing me anymore. I started my own company.

I enjoy the days when you come in and make special things to decorate my office. As I watch you blossom, I see a humble young lady who never forgets the unfortunate and is always willing to share or even give up what is hers to someone else to bring them happiness. At Christmas, when we ring bells for the Salvation Army, you have remarked that it always seems to be those with less that put money in the pot. That is because they know what it is like to be without. But they also know that there is always someone with less than they have.

Being a mom is the most rewarding thing I have ever decided to do. I know I can't always protect you and keep you out of harm's way, but know that you have the greatest thing on earth that even money cannot buy—the love of your family. My lesson for you that I learned from our past dealings with poverty is to always remember to be kind to others no matter what or who they are. Never take anything for granted. And always tell yourself that you can make it. You can make it! These are the gems that our tough times have taught us. Never forget them.

I couldn't be prouder of you. It's so rewarding to know in my heart that you will not experience as much of the bad when you become an adult because of what we have overcome in your childhood.

Thank you for giving me the things I needed to be a strong mother—your love and support. I love you, Boog!

LOVE,

MOM

TO MY BABY GIRL,

I don't know where to start 'cause I have so much that I want to say. I'll start with "I love you." That is my inspiration for life. When you were only eight months old, your mom went back to drugs. I was searching for some relief from the grief that haunted me. You were oh so small. Such an innocence. One I wish would never change. I fear for your innocence. I fear for you.

When I was in a coma, drug induced, the one dream I can remember and always will remember is your soft sweet smile and your innocent eyes when I last held you. When the angel came to me in my dream and asked me if I was ready to go, I said, "Not yet, my baby girl needs me. I can't leave her just yet." The dream came to me again, only now I know it wasn't a dream. I wasn't ready to die. I couldn't leave you with so much to learn.

I don't want for you the same bad things I did to me. I want to be there for you to guide you so that you might not make those same mistakes. As I know I can't stop you from trying drugs, I can share with you the brutal life of a drug addict, the person I was, the nightmare I lived and almost died for.

I remember the smile on your face and how your eyes lit up when Grandma brought you to the hospital the day I came out of the coma. As soon as you saw me, you reached out to me saying, "Mama." I stretched out my arms to grab you as you jumped from Grandma's arms to mine. I felt the minute that you were in my arms that I had been given another chance at life. Oh my baby, Miriah, what would you have done if your mama had died that night, died a junkie? How could you have grown up and told your friends why you had no mom? The shame I would have left you to face, a betrayal of the heart, my baby girl.

PAMELA, WHO IS SERVING TIME FOR A DRUG-RELATED CRIME AND IS SOON TO BE PAROLED, ADDRESSES THE HOPES SHE HAS FOR THE DAYS AHEAD WITH HER DAUGHTER.

18

I have learned from my pain that what I wish for you is not to suffer the indignities of a drug addict, as I did. I believe your angel had a purpose for us. I will always protect you from my evil past by explaining to you as I watch you grow how you almost lost me that night. My fears of you following in those same footsteps is what brought me back into this world, to guide you towards another path in life. When you are old enough to understand, you and I will sit down together and read this letter, only in hopes that you will know that you are my baby girl and that my love for you is and was my inspiration for life. You were all the reason in the world for me to stop doing drugs, and I hope to inspire you not to try drugs, also.

I LOVE YOU, MIRIAH JEAN,

MAMA

DEAR JULIE,

The unbelievable fact that your sister was taken away from you by such an untimely death and left you as an only child still makes me very, very sad. The burden you took upon yourself to be both Arabelle and Julie was just too much for you. Through it all you have grown so very much.

But where does it all begin . . . ? Early childhood taught me if I am only very good, nothing bad will happen to me. If I only please everybody, I will be loved. It seemed to work for me for a long time. Then bad things did happen. On second thought, to conceive Arabelle in love was not bad at all. At that time in my life I discovered that life requires us to make choices. It was my choice to have a baby out of wed-lock at a time when this was considered shameful and wrong. Not only was that shame put on me but also on my parents. However, my deci-sion rewarded me with a beautiful baby girl. I aston-ished myself when I named her so out of the ordinary, Arabelle. As we know, she was a very spe-cial human being, born for a reason—to bring joy and sadness and growth.

URSULA, WHOSE DAUGHTER ARABELLE WAS KILLED AT AGE 15 BY A DRUNK DRIVER, WRITES OF THE JOY ARABELLE BROUGHT TO HER LIFE AND HER DAUGHTER JULIE'S AND OF THE CONTINUED JOY SHE FINDS IN JULIE.

Arabelle, if you were here today I would tell you of the love I had for you. You taught me so much in the short time you were mine. From you I learned how to live the phrase, "If you can't say anything nice about someone, then don't say anything at all." You loved life and lived it, and I discovered from you that even though life does not unfold the way one has mapped it out, it can still be all right simply by making the choice to move forward. Not that we should forget the past—remembering is beautiful, but not to dwell on all the injustices that life has to dish out. For this I thank you.

Julie, if there is anything I could pass on to you it would be this: As I started out saying, life is a series of choices we make. You seem to live by this already. But I caution you, there will be very difficult decisions along the way. Use sound judgment. If you listen to your inner voice, your heart will give you the answer. Sometimes that requires patience and time, so be very still so that you can hear yourself.

As a mother you have honored me, and it fills me with warmth and gratitude that you are my daughter.

MY LOVE TO YOU ALWAYS,

MUM

My dear Shelley,

I can still remember the joy of holding you in my arms for the first time. You were such a tiny baby, but as I held you close, you suddenly reminded me of what a big miracle you were.

Two months before you were born, the doctors informed me of some serious health complications which had developed during my pregnancy. They said you had stopped growing inside me. I was advised to deliver you early in order to prevent any further complications. They warned me, however, that an early delivery might bring about even more complications. I remember the fear which overcame me that day as I tried to make an important decision.

SANDRA, WHOSE DAUGHTER WAS BORN WITH SPINA BIFIDA AND BRAIN DAMAGE, ACKNOWLEDGES THE MIRACLE OF HER DAUGHTER'S BIRTH AND THE CONTINUED CHALLENGES BOTH MUST FACE.

I decided to face my fear with faith and carry you the full term of my pregnancy, despite what the doctors had told me . . . and now here you were in my arms, truly a miracle, my precious gift from God. After being advised by the doctors to keep you in the hospital a few days longer because of your size (four pounds), I left for home without you. It was so hard leaving the hospital without you. I felt so cheated, left out, and empty. As a single mom, I had to face those feelings alone, finding my own strength and courage! That week, waiting, seemed like an eternity.

I soon had you home with me and began to find out what motherhood was all about. The sleepless nights and many tears we cried seemed to bring about the beginning of a special bond between us. Then one day you laughed for the first time, and I knew you had discovered that life held within it a certain joy that surrounded our pain and sorrows. Nine months later we would visit the same hospital where we first began our journey of life together. After several tests I was told by a specialist that you were born with spina bifida and brain damage. You would be slow at learning and possibly never be able to walk because of the opening in your spine.

I was devastated and in shock. How could this be? How would I be able to find the strength and courage to raise this kind of child who needed so much of my help? Guilt, fear, helplessness, sorrow, and many disappointments invaded my life.

For the next two years you underwent many tests. During this time I felt as if I'd been put through a few tests of my own. I tried hard to replace my guilt with acceptance, my fear with courage and faith, my helplessness with hard work, my sorrow with joy, and my many disappointments with hope for our future.

I discovered that my love for you was unconditional. But could my love for you win the many battles we were faced with? Would love be able to go beyond the boundaries when everything else seemed to fail? I believed in my heart it could. After months

of tears and prayers, love did go beyond the boundaries. You took your first step, the first step of many you would take towards the challenges you'd face.

I know it has not been easy for you. I know there have been times in your life when you have felt cheated and alone, when others would not include you because you were different. You have been fearful and in doubt when attempting to do the things you could not do without struggle, sad when you were made fun of because of who you were. The road ahead will be a challenging one for you. There are going to be times you will have to make difficult decisions. There will be times when fear and doubt, helplessness, sorrow, and many disappointments will invade your life as it did mine.

My advice to you would be to make decisions without fear or doubt, but with faith as your guide. Let the helplessness you feel at times turn into good judgment and motivate you to work a little harder. But most important of all, let love go beyond the boundaries. I believe that love conquers all!

Thank you, Shelley, for all the joy you have brought to me in my life, your unfailing love so freely given to me and others. I will support you and love you as you continue to conquer the challenges you face in your journey of life.

LOVE ALWAYS AND FOREVER,

MOM

DEAR DIANNE,

*E*ach of us has plans and dreams throughout our lives. My life and dreams had been fulfilled until March 4, 1987. My first choice was to be married, be a homemaker, and have children. I had been so totally blessed.

I first met my special guy, "my prince," in 1942. Our lives together were filled with so many interests. We spent time outdoors. Your dad was a real outdoor man, enjoying hunting, fishing, hiking, and, oh yes, motorcycles. Remember how you and your brother enjoyed riding in the sidecar?

It was a beautiful, sunny early spring day in March when Daddy went for a hike after work. He exercised daily, so this was nothing unusual for him to do. At about 5:15 that afternoon, I was standing in the kitchen when I had a strange pain in my chest and gasped for a breath. I remember thinking, I'll tell Daddy about this when he gets home. Daddy was always prompt, so when he did not return by 5:45, I just knew something was wrong. By this time it was dark and I knew I needed to go look for him. I called friends from the church and said, "Jay is lost." (Of course he wasn't lost. He knew every inch of that mountain.) At least 30 people joined in on the search.

I went home at about 11:00 P.M. to phone you. You told me to get lots of warm clothes to take back to the mountain with me because Daddy would be cold and he could get pneumonia.

Next morning friends would not let me go search! At 9:15 A.M. our pastor came to tell me, "We found Jay; he has gone to heaven." What a shock! I needed and wanted to see him. I convinced someone to take me. There he lay with a surprised and almost happy look on his face, and his hands in such a position that, had he been sitting or standing, would have been open and raised toward heaven. They said that Daddy had died at about 5:15 P.M. from a heart attack.

Since that day in 1987, each day has been terribly long and lonely. The day never ends, and then the night never ends. I am told that life goes on. It's true, we do exist, but I lost my husband and my best friend, and I am finding it to be a very hard adjustment to make.

I would never make it without your love and caring, Dianne. I find such comfort in you. It is always good to hear your voice or see your face. You are so much like your dad. People have even asked me if your likeness to him is hard for me. "Oh no," I say. "It is very comforting." I know I must not be good company sometimes and that I ask the same questions over and over, but you have been patient and supportive and I am truly thankful for you. I know you miss your dad very much, and I hope that I am able to offer you comfort, too.

EUNICE SPEAKS OF LOSING HER HUSBAND AND LIFE PARTNER OF MORE THAN 40 YEARS.

Dianne, I spend so much time looking back. Daddy and I had a full life together. Yet now there is such emptiness. I can't help but think of your future, and I want to encourage you to plan wisely. Talk to your husband about finances, medical decisions that may arise, and decisions that must be made if one or both of you were to die in an untimely way. Tell each other how much you love each other, and celebrate each day you have together. The loss of a husband is so significant, but if you are in the dark about how to handle yourself, then the devastation is almost impossible to bear. Please let me be of help to you if I can.

I LOVE YOU LOTS,

MOTHER

DEAR DAN DAN ("Good Luck" in Chinese),

*L*ast night I called you in China, and you asked me, "Mom, when are you going to come back?" I could not help crying. When? I don't know and I am desperate to know. Also, recently, whenever I call you and tell you that I love you, you start to question. "Since you are always telling me that you love me, why don't you come back to me?" I am speechless. You're only six years old, and this year has been so difficult for you. I can't expect you to understand that I am away from you because I am trying to create a better future for you and for myself.

It has been a year since I left you in China to come to America to study and work. Many people have asked me if I like America or not. I always tell them that being a woman, I can be myself on

this piece of land. That is also the reason why I have been trying so hard to get you over here. I want you to fully develop yourself to be yourself.

You might be curious now. What stopped me from being myself back in China? The reason is China's traditional and cultural values. In Chinese culture, women historically were considered property of men. Five thousand years of feudalism has developed a whole system of oppressing women. In the Song dynasty the custom reached its peak with the establishment of the Three Obediences theory. The obediences: at home, be obedient to your father; in wedlock, be obedient to your husband; in widowhood, be obedient to your

AFTER LEAVING HER SIX-YEAR-OLD DAUGHTER IN CHINA TO FIND A BETTER FUTURE FOR THEM, LULIN REALIZES THAT, FOR MANY REASONS, HER PLACE IS WITH HER DAUGHTER.

son. This theory passed down from generation to generation and became deeply rooted in the minds of the Chinese people. The woman's main goal was to meet the needs of her husband and family, never herself. I was born into a family that had these values. Sons were highly valued; daughters were not.

I came to America with a dream of a better life, of new opportunities, of more choices, and, especially, of becoming myself. Since I have been in America, I have done research in women's studies. I have given lectures about Chinese history, culture, and the life of women in China. I have done work in translation and in the interpretation of the Chinese language.

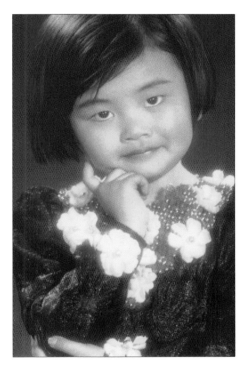

However, I realized that part of who I am is my love for you and my relationship with you. Without you, my dream is not complete. I see a beautiful sunset, but I am still sad. I take a walk and can't appreciate the beauty around me. Each season seems gray.

Dan Dan, I am coming home to you soon. I realize now that no matter where we are, we have to be together. All I want is to be there for you with my eyes opened, my mind enriched. I want to be with you so I can teach you English, help you with homework. Most of all, I want to share with you what I have learned in America.

I know that when I return home I will face many hardships. But I feel ready to make us a family and to share with your father what I learned in America. In the Chinese culture it is impossible for children to survive when parents are divorced. The child will lose face. I do not want this for you. So, no matter what the consequences, it is my responsibility to be with your father so that you have a whole family.

I will be home soon!

LOVE,

MOM

DEAR MOLLY,

My heart was filled with joy when I found out I was pregnant with you, and my prayers were answered when you were born healthy. Now you are growing up to be a fine young girl. You have such a spirit for life and are willing to try and experience many things. I hope that spirit never diminishes. There is so much I want for you and your life.

There is nothing more important to me than to let you know how precious you are. My prayer is that you come to know God and that you will learn those characteristics that are worthy of possessing: love, servanthood, forgiveness, honesty, sincerity . . . I can only hope that I can be an example to you.

I hope you have a love in your heart for the many wonderful things in this world you will see and for the different kinds of people you will meet. I hope you believe in yourself as much as I do and believe in how wonderful you are regardless of your appearance. I hope you will look deep inside your heart at what you have done and know it was good and you did your best.

AMY, A DWARF WHOSE DAUGHTER WILL BE AVERAGE SIZE, WRITES OF HER EXPERIENCES AND OF PERSEVERING AND ACCEPTING DIFFERENCES.

It took me a long time to believe in who I was, or at least to show it on the outside. It was not until later in my life that I thought of myself as okay and not someone that was different and didn't belong. I knew I belonged to my family and a few close friends, but not too much else. I didn't think much about being born an achondroplasia dwarf. It was not a big deal until I got to school and appearances seemed to matter more and more.

It was tough to overcome people's attitudes and impressions. I wasn't always good at not letting negative feelings affect me so much. Your grandma and grandpa always taught me to believe in myself, that I could do anything I set my mind to regardless of what people thought. I often believed it in the inside but did not show it on the outside.

I tried to convince myself that it didn't matter that I was sometimes the last one picked for games, or thought of as an acquaintance instead of someone's close friend, or never asked out on a date. I never really understood why. I always thought of myself as a pretty good person, just short. However, to others I was different.

I made myself try new things, like trying out for the pompom squad (I didn't make it) and the marching band (I was in this for three years). I really felt that I would never get married or have children, even when I joined the organization of Little People of America and met so many dwarfs like me. I still thought of myself as different from them. I couldn't believe I looked like that.

I think I stopped dwelling on how different I was when I started college. I soon realized that I could do so many things, the same things that others did, perhaps just a little differently. People seemed more mature, more open and accepting. People's think-

ing about me being short became more second nature. It was tough finding that first job, but it got easier as time went on.

Deep down inside I never gave up hope. Eventually I met your father through the Little People of America organization, and I was given the greatest gifts: being a mom to you, your brothers, and the new baby on the way.

Know that you are always loved. Never give up trying things no matter what others think or tell you. Believe in yourself and never give less than your best. You will make mistakes and fall down sometimes, but I hope you have the belief in yourself to pick yourself up and continue on.

You will encounter many different kinds of people. Sometimes it will be hard to look beyond appearances because that is what we tend to see first. Don't stop there! Get to know people. Look

into their hearts, their attitudes, their actions. These are the characteristics that will let you know who someone is. You will never know what you are missing if you look at appearances only.

I LOVE YOU WITH ALL MY HEART!

MOM

M Y   D E A R E S T   D A U G H T E R ,

When you were born at Good Samaritan Hospital, I was so overjoyed I could hardly contain myself. A lovely little six-pound girl after back-to-back nine-and-a-half-pound boys. I was sure that God had smiled favorably on me!

Over the years, watching you grow from a left-handed tomboy and blossom into a beautiful young lady was more joyful than I had hoped for. And further, you were spunky! Not only were you talented, but what an achiever! Always tops in student government, an honor student, and well loved by teachers and students. This was not easy because of prejudice— there were only two or three black families in the area, and I know you had definite challenges.

Forgive me for raising you to be "color-blind." I did not want you to suffer the pain of discrimination, nor did I want

to set limits on your achievements because of issues related to race. I wanted you to simply spread your wings and fly. And soar you did! By our hard work and example, your father and I wanted to show you that "where there is a will, there is a way" and that you can do anything you set your mind to. I'm sure you remember me saying over and over again while you were growing up, "With God's help, all things are possible."

I particularly remember the pain and inadequacy I felt, and the disappointment I'm sure you felt, when I had to send you back to college one semester with only $6 in your pocket to pay for tuition. It was all I had. That day, the only advice I could give you was to go see the dean of women and see if she could find some way to help you. You didn't like the idea, but you didn't have a choice. Your faith and perseverance enabled you to qualify for more scholarship money; and of all my children I was the proudest of you when you graduated from the University of Oregon. Who would have guessed that your love for the written word and your passion for justice would have placed you in the higher-education arena, leading the way to open the doors for under-represented minorities and students who were not financially able to go to college.

GENEVA CONVEYS A MESSAGE OF PRIDE IN HER DAUGHTER'S MANY ACCOMPLISHMENTS.

As a mature mother and now single parent of one son, my only grandson, you have amazed me with your strength and abilities to cope with some devastating relationships and health challenges that would have surely thrown me for a loop. I am still getting to know and understand you in all of your glory. In the past, where I could not be there for you emotionally in times of stress and distress, God has now given me this opportunity to be with you—now that you have returned from the East and have been living with me. Sometimes, I'm not quite sure how to best use this blessing, but I know you know that I am here for you. I am so very proud of you.

BUNDLES OF LOVE AND KISSES,
MOTHER

DEAR JESSICA,

*Y*ou are becoming a young woman and there is so much I want to say. It is hard to find the words or time in our everyday life to tell you all the things I want you to know. I can only hope that we continue to be friends as well as family so that we will always openly communicate.

There is nothing I wouldn't do to keep you from harm. I want to keep you from ever hurting, but to do that would mean keeping you from the learning experiences that come with pain and failures. Learning brings joy and is the ultimate purpose of our being. We are here to learn and grow. Our minds, bodies, and souls cry out to know and be more. Follow that yearning. Learn all that you can. Don't be afraid to take risks, but be aware of what those risks are before you decide to act.

AFTER HER BATTLE WITH ADDICTION, LINDA HOPES TO HELP HER DAUGHTER AND OTHER WOMEN REALIZE THE GOAL OF SELF-SUFFICIENCY.

So often in your young life you've seen me take risks and make foolish mistakes that caused such heartache because I didn't weigh the possible outcomes. My battles with addiction and selfishness caused disruption in your life. I wish we had the opportunity to start over again so you could experience me as a real mother.

I know that the trials of the past caused you to grow up quickly. For you, childhood was filled with having to deal with very adult issues and feelings. You had to be sensible and smart. You are intelligent and discerning, so much so that at times I forget how young you are. Be young, though! It's okay to be silly, to cry, to be confused, and to not know the answers. Learn this now because the questions get harder and harder in life and the only real answer is to have faith in yourself to get through whatever you are facing. Take one thing at a time and give yourself a break for the things you can't do yet. If you need to do them, there will be a way in time.

I hope you know how much I love you, how beautiful you are, and how happy and proud I am to be your mom. I want to give you all the best, and there is so much it seems I can't. There is a lesson, though, in how we are learning to know our limitations and find joy in what we do have. We struggle financially. We grieve the loss of your father and the death of your stepdad. We face the challenges of school, work, and family, but we do it together—there is no better way. We are learning how to give, not out of excess, but out of sharing, because of our understanding of being in need. We are blessed with faith that all our needs will be provided for and are shown miraculously time and time again that this is true. We need only be willing to help our neighbors, to be a friend, and to believe.

The journey of life is best shared with people who love and accept you. Seek out and be this type of person throughout your own journey. The choices you make about who accompanies you in life have a profound influence on how you feel about yourself. You cannot afford to have anyone distort your belief that you are beneficial and valuable to the world. You have special talents and gifts that no one else has. You are unique, one of a kind, loved and priceless. Anyone who would try to make you believe otherwise is a liar or sick themselves. Hold on to your identity, your dignity, and your self-respect. These things are the only real possessions you have.

I have faith in you. I believe you will accomplish more than either of us can imagine. Already you have survived and blossomed in an environment that might have caused others to give up. I hope you will be able to continue to turn the difficulties in your life into lessons. I desperately want to be a worthy teacher, friend, and mother. I look forward to so much with you that it's hard sometimes to let go and let you be with others. You are coming into a really hard set of transitions in your life, and I hope that I can be a shoulder to cry on and an ear for listening, now and always.

I LOVE YOU,

MOM

DEAREST HALEY AND LAUREN,

The hardest thing I have ever done was to leave your father. In the 14 years we were married I stayed, trying to make it work because I wanted to protect you. I wanted to provide you with a healthy, intact family. What I realized was that it was damaging to you, to me, to all of us. In fear I left, all of our necessary belongings hurriedly thrown into boxes, and the three of us were on our own. I was terrified, and yet knew that I had made the right choice. I still remember hearing the whisper of God saying, "You have done all you can. It's okay to leave now."

I could have chosen to have others take care of us—friends, my parents and family. But I wanted you to see a strong female role model, someone who could take care of herself and her two young daughters and would do whatever it took to provide a loving and supportive family in spite of it all. I remember our first days alone in our condominium, tearing down wallpaper, creating a home that was ours. It felt so good to tuck you in bed at night, exhausted from a full day at work, scooping you up at daycare, homework, dinner, reading, bedtime rituals, and yet filled with love and hope for the first time in a very long time.

MOLLY WRITES ABOUT THE DIFFICULT CHOICE TO LEAVE A LONG-TERM MARRIAGE AND THE JOY AND STRENGTH FOUND IN THE MIDST OF BEING A SINGLE PARENT.

I sought counseling for all of us, so that we could deal with the very real emotions that occur when a family is torn apart. Children are often left to fend for themselves when a divorce occurs while the parents nurse their own wounds. Because of the place that you hold in my life, and the love and commitment I have for the two of you, I never let you do that. Do you remember the divorce recovery group for children we started? As hard as that all was, and as much as it would have been so much easier to just not talk about it, I chose not to do that. More importantly, you made the same choice. I am so proud of you both for being willing to take on the pain and hard work that healing often takes.

As time went on we moved more than once to get into better neighborhoods and schools. Each move required you to leave behind friends, teachers, and all that had become familiar. Your courage and trust were my greatest inspiration. I will never forget renting our little white "cottage." We showed up to see it and I was the only single parent among the crowd that had come, and a single woman at that. I was sure the landlord would never rent it to us when she obviously had better candidates. Not you! You took me into the back bedroom and said, "Mom, this is it! We just know it." The next day the landlord

34

called and said that she had been a single parent at one time and wished someone had given her a break. She gave us a break and we moved in. Two years later we bought our own house. Do you remember how proud we all were? I wouldn't trade those years for anything.

Today you stand on the brink of independence. Together we are facing the perils of adolescence with hope, courage, love, and the same strength and commitment that saw us through the struggles of the past years. There is nothing that will come your way that you will not be able to handle. You've been through the fire and came out not only surviving but thriving. You are strong, loving, compassionate, and capable. No one can take that away from you.

Know that I am your greatest ally and fan. I will continue to applaud at your victories and walk with you through trials and mistakes. I look in your faces and am proud of who we are—who you are as a result of being my daughters—and even more, proud of who I am because of the honor and privilege of being your mother.

I'LL LOVE YOU FOREVER,

MAMA

M Y   D A U G H T E R ,

*W*ords cannot possibly express the love that I have for you. But I believe that you will come to understand the depth of love that I have felt for you from the time I first became aware of your presence until today as you read this letter for the first time.

You came into this world surrounded on all sides not only by my love, and that of very special friends, but also by my mother, your grandmother. Although you have never met her, she loves you deeply and counts you among her grandchildren as surely as those who benefit from her presence. Rather than having less, you had an abundance of love, more than so many in this world.

The most precious memories of my life will be the moments I had to hold and love you. I was encouraged by many in the hospital not to do so—to have you taken away from me as soon as you were born, so that I would not have to experience the increased pain of our separation. How grateful I am that I did not heed the advice. For three days I held you, fed you, prayed for you, and became forever connected to you. I looked into your eyes and memorized every detail of your

THIS MOTHER WRITES ABOUT HER DECISION TO GIVE UP HER DAUGHTER FOR ADOPTION AND REMEMBERS THE FIRST FEW DAYS THEY SPENT TOGETHER.

tiny life. To give up something as precious and beautiful as you were to me is never without pain. But along with that pain I understood as never before that the heart of love is giving. For me that meant giving up the opportunity to be your mother. I chose to give you to a family that I felt would offer you a life that I could not. This is the highest form of love that I could give you.

As you read this letter, I believe that you have been part of a family where you have been nurtured and loved for who you are, and have been able to grow into all that you are capable of becoming. There are no mistakes in life. I believe that everything works together for good and am thankful to have had an active part in sending you on your way.

Know always that you are loved with all the depth of a mother's heart, and that there is a place in my heart that belongs only to you.

I LOVE YOU,

MOM

MY DEAR DAUGHTERS,

I want to thank you for teaching me what a wonderful thing it is to be a mother. As you know, I didn't start out parenting you with much of an understanding of how a family is supposed to work. But we managed to teach each other, and I will be forever grateful.

I wasn't born deaf. When I was about 10 months old I got very sick with whooping cough. As a result I lost my hearing. As a very young child I lived at the Salem School for the Deaf. I learned how to use sign language, write English, and interact with people. But growing up deaf, this was all I really knew. I knew nothing much about what life was like in the outside world.

I went home on holidays to visit my family. Due to my limited contact, though, they felt more like friends than family. My parents never gave me any advice about having a family of my own. I didn't really know that deaf people could be married or have children. I didn't know any deaf adults outside of the school.

I met your father at the deaf school. We married in 1960. Rosalyn, you were born December 15, 1962. We both felt so

awkward, being around a crying baby for the first time. I started to teach you sign language right away. It was the only language I had to communicate with my hearing daughter. I always worried about your own speech development, though, so I asked family and friends to communicate with you every chance they had.

I remember when you, Rosalyn, were four years old. A friend of ours overdosed on some pills. I tried my best to help you call 911 for an ambulance. I did CPR and tried to sign to you at the same time. This was very hard for me. But, my daughter, that day you were a hero.

Two years after your birth, Rosalyn, your sister, Pam, was born. I felt so very blessed. But it wasn't easy for us. I guess it isn't easy for any mom and daughter. Our situation was unique, though. You became my teachers as much as I was yours. We learned how to work out frustrations, sadness, and differences with patience. Because of our hard work you are my closest friends. We understand each other's feelings, keep secrets for one another, and communicate constantly.

JANELLA, WHO IS DEAF BUT WHO HAS TWO HEARING DAUGHTERS, TELLS OF LEARNING TO LIVE IN BOTH THE DEAF AND HEARING WORLDS.

I am so proud of both of you and the work you do for the deaf community. You both have such big hearts, and I know that sign language is something you value and will pass on to future generations of our family. What a joy it is to communicate with my grandchildren through sign language.

I don't think of myself as handicapped. I feel normal. I owe that to my hearing daughters. You have lived and learned in the hearing and the deaf communities and you have included me in both. I am so thankful for the good life we've had and the good memories we share.

LOVE,

MOM

DEAR JODIE,

I am sitting here by the fire looking at you recovering from an illness. I have been thinking about a lot of things since my father died two weeks ago. There are so many thoughts I would like to pass on . . . but here is just one.

In my life I have often tried to avoid things that are hard. Sometimes I think you do, too. Yet, for me, I have discovered that most of the things that have enriched my life have some hard parts to them, good things like bushwalking, being married, or having children (you know the hard work that involves because you were there when your brother and sister were born!). Let me share a story with you.

When you were three months old your dad and I took you on a two-week bushwalk into the wilderness in southwest Tasmania. Civilization was a week's walk away, and we had to carry in our backpacks everything we needed. You didn't need much as you were fully breast-fed and you slept on the ground in a tent under your father's down jacket for warmth. You only had one change of clothes. It didn't matter if you got dirty in the bush!

One day we were walking in heavy rain all day. You were dry, in a papoose carrier nestled against my chest and underneath my raincoat. It was cold, with rain teeming into my face and soaking through my overpants as they rubbed against wet undergrowth. I was very uncomfortable. There was nowhere to stop and no shelter on the windswept button-grass plains. The only thing to do was to keep walking in order to keep warm.

SUSAN ILLUSTRATES THE NEED TO EMBRACE THE DIFFICULT CIRCUMSTANCES AND CHOICES THAT ARE PART OF LIFE.

It had to happen eventually; your quiet cries came from beneath my rain-jacket. You needed a feed. There was no choice but to sit in the pouring rain on a wet log with my wet feet and breast-feed you for 15 minutes. You were as dry and secure as a baby joey in the mother kangaroo's pouch, suckling while oblivious to the rest of the world. It was cold and uncomfortable but needed to be done.

I will never forget that walk and that miserable moment on the wet log. Yet, I remember it now as a precious moment I had with you, sheltering you from the rain and the cold. That walk and time of closeness with you in the wilderness was unforgettable and deeply satisfying. You were a new human being. Your life at that time was virtually unaffected by the world, just like the area in which we had walked.

You know, Jodie, I think most of the things I value or that have helped me grow have had elements of pain or hard work. I want to share this with you so you don't miss out on good things just because they are hard. You are growing up in a culture which tells you to avoid the uncomfortable things—buy a softer bed, get another effort-saving appliance, disband your relationships that are a bit difficult or costly.

Sometimes the difficult experiences in life come not by choice. When I was 10 like you are now I began to steal money from my mum's drawer to give to friends at school. I was trying to buy their friendship. I also told big stories about my dad being an important policeman and solving crimes.

I was lying and stealing because I was insecure about my family. You see, Dad had a mental illness—schizophrenia. He couldn't do a normal job or even simple things around the house. I knew something was wrong, but no one ever talked about it. Mental illness was an uncomfortable, painful, hard-work thing to deal with. So everybody avoided talking about it. I don't think I heard the word *schizophrenia* until I was at the university. The cost of not facing this problem in our family was high. I felt we were somehow different or inadequate. I was very hesitant about inviting friends over. It affected my confidence in many ways.

It is all right now. I know all about it and have talked about it with friends and family. The honesty and trust that flowed when we dealt with it have been a great encouragement to me. I don't feel bad or ashamed about Dad being sick. But so many years were confusing and sad for me when I didn't understand. Sure, it was hard work to deal with it and I cried a lot, but I'm a much more complete person since I've done that hard work.

Writing this has just made me fill up with love for you. It is such a privilege to grow with you, Jodie. I will try to encourage you to face up to hard things, and please will you encourage me to do the same?

L O V E ,

M O M

*D*EAR *C*HILDREN,

I am 71, semi-retired, and at my age one is apt to reflect on one's life. I realize now that my generation, who were adults in World War II, will soon be gone.

When the Netherlands were invaded by Nazis, my grandparents were about my age now and were living with my family in Utrecht. Like most Jews in the country they were ordered to go to Amsterdam, but my father was able to get a permit

for them to stay with us "until further notice," as most permits read. After a few months we were warned by good friends that the SS was carrying out orders to round up the elderly and take them to Amsterdam. We had no time to find a hiding place, so we had to think fast about what we could do to save them, at least for that day.

THIS MOTHER WHO LIVED THROUGH YEARS IN A CONCENTRATION CAMP IN HOLLAND CONVEYS STRENGTH, COURAGE, AND THE WILL TO SURVIVE.

We came up with a plan to stage a "sick" scene. The Germans did not like sick people, especially if they thought the disease might be communicable. My mother, who was a Red Cross nurse, put on her uniform and gathered ether, syringes, and Lysol to set the stage. My grandparents were to play very, very sick. We rehearsed quickly as we didn't know when the SS would come. About an hour later there were two black-booted, green-uniformed monsters ringing the bell and banging on the door. The act was then set in motion. All of the actors did great, my mother running around with medicine and my grand-parents moaning and groaning. The soldiers asked what was wrong with them, and my mother said it was probably dysentery. They quickly left the house. As soon as they left we laughed until tears ran over our faces. We celebrated prematurely. They returned. Luckily, most of the sickroom was still intact. So the show went on again, very convincingly. Again it worked and the SS left.

My grandparents had a few more weeks' respite from their fate. They finally had to obey and were transported to Amsterdam. Once there, they were taken, along with all the other old people, to the Amsterdam Theater, where they were packed together in a holding pattern, waiting for transport to ???? Of course, no one could imagine what was in store for them.

I remember that we received a postcard, thrown out of the train and mailed by friendly people. My grandparents wrote that even though they would be very lonely for us all, they would be all right. We should not worry because they could make themselves very useful. My grandfather could peel potatoes and my grandmother was excellent at darning socks.

They wrote this postcard on the train to Auschwitz. They had no concept of the graveness of the situation. Neither did we. I have since learned that they were gassed to death in Auschwitz just a few days after leaving Holland.

The war and experiences like this one very much shaped my attitude towards life. I am grateful you did not have to go through those. Certainly your life's experiences will not parallel mine. But there will be times when your life seems so difficult that you think you can't go on. Life does that to all of us. I learned that when I thought I could go no further, I could always find the strength to go on just a little more. If everything else fails, use your inner strength, fortified with faith and wisdom gathered along the way.

I feel so very fortunate to know you all! Count your blessings, and when you feel low, do something constructive, do something for somebody else. When you have to make difficult decisions about important matters, sleep on it, listen to your heart and gut feelings! Seek support from those who love you and draw strength from the knowledge that my love is always with you. I hope you will have many blessings and happiness.

MOTHER

DEAR JENNA AND KRISTEN,

*I*t is through no fault of our own that the three of us have been severed from the generations of women that were to be forever linked to us. My birth mother at age 22 could not possibly have known the far-reaching implications of her decision to relinquish me at birth. She could not have imagined the emptiness I have lived with on a daily basis. She did not realize that, even in childhood, I would sink into deep despair because of not feeling like I "belonged" anywhere on this earth. I believe it would have broken her heart to realize that I would spend a lifetime fighting to believe in my intrinsic goodness and against the notion that I must have done something terribly wrong and that people will always leave me. I can forgive my birth mother only because I believe she did not understand that by severing herself from me, she took my roots, the faces and stories of my grandmothers, and my sense of being connected in this world.

KATHRYN REVEALS THE PAIN SHE HAS EXPERIENCED BECAUSE SHE DID NOT GROW UP IN HER BIRTH FAMILY AND ENCOURAGES HER DAUGHTERS TO REMEMBER THE IMPORTANCE OF FAMILY CONNECTION.

The universe brings its own form of salve to our wounds, which brings me to the two of you. You were conceived with a man who has loved and stood by me for 19 years and carried in the warmth of my womb. You were wanted and planned for. As little girls you loved to hear the stories about my pregnancies with you. I realize now that I stressed the part about you being *wanted* at each telling of the story.

Jenna, nearly 16 years ago you entered this world as the first human being I had ever seen that shared my blood. I looked into your eyes when the nurse handed you to me and asked in amazement, "Where have I seen those eyes?" For the first time in my life, I felt a soul connection to another person. On a daily basis, I recognize the many ways we are alike: the shape of our faces, the strength of our legs, our stubbornness. Our bond is forever a very special one.

Kristen, my tenderhearted daughter, you were born two and a half years after your sister. When the doctor removed you from my body, I could hardly believe that I was being blessed with another daughter. Our love of nature runs so deeply. Your sense of humor graces my life, and I still marvel that our fingers (and even our fingernails) could match so exactly.

Now I realize that I needed both of you to begin the healing of my own shattered heart. From the moment I knew I was pregnant, I loved you deeply in the way I had longed for from my birth mother. I have not been a perfect mother, but I have always cherished you, guided you, believed in you, and stood by you. It is the promise I made at your births. It is the promise I make to you for the rest of my life.

I accept the honor of being the new matriarch in our family, even though I am only 40 and have had no role models. I will trust my instincts, however, as they have proven to be a great source of guidance. Perhaps such things are passed on genetically, which would mean we can never be totally severed from our ancestors, even if we have never seen their faces. Accepting myself as I am and watching the two of you mature in adolescence has convinced me that we came from a strong stalk of women. Let us never forget the importance of connection.

Thank you for the healing you have brought to my life. I am forever grateful.

WITH LOVE,

MOM

MY DAUGHTERS,

I f only I could protect you from the things you must face, the things you must learn. This living is difficult and there will be many trials. I hardly feel qualified to instruct you, advise you, mother you, but seeing as how I have been thrust, albeit willingly, into this position, I shall do what every mother does: my best.

So many lessons will you face. I am certain I could fill page upon page with motherly ramblings about sharing, being true to yourself, and being a good person. And while those things are truly important, there is one thing I have learned that surpasses all others. Let me tell you a story:

DAWN SPEAKS OF HER FATHER'S SUICIDE AND OF THE IMPORTANCE OF EXPRESSING LOVE AND FORGIVENESS.

Your grandfather, my father, Papa to you, was only 52 when he died. You were small children then and hardly remember him. He led a difficult though illustrious life. I was his first daughter, born when he and my mother were only 19. I know he

tried as best he could to be a good father to me, and for the most part he was, but he was human. Papa was an alcoholic. Not the door slamming, name calling, punch throwing type. Just your ordinary "one-beer-too-many" variety that quietly fell into peaceful slumber while the world crashed down around him.

My mom did the best she knew how raising my sisters and me. I know now how frustrating it was dealing with us when Dad was drinking. Needless to say, neither he nor my mom were able to give us the depth of love my sisters and I so craved. Sometimes, I hated my father. I hated him for making my mom cry. I hated him for not being there when I needed him. I hated him for getting drunk at public functions and embarrassing himself and our family. Most of all, I hated him for not loving me, or so I thought.

There were times, rough times, when my dad and I did not speak to each other. I had always felt that he thought I had disappointed him and the family. I also felt he had not been allowing me to make my own decisions. The lack of communication was difficult, especially for my mother who was caught in the middle of two very stubborn individuals. Eventually, once I had finally learned to live on my own, he and I came to a peaceful resolution. No, I would never be the daughter he had dreamed I would be, the doctor, the professional woman . . . and he would never be the dad I had wanted him to be, perfect, immortal, not human. But it was okay. We learned to accept and love each other. He also learned to stop drinking. He was sober the last eight years of his life. In those eight years, he and I came full circle. We were no longer adversaries. We became friends.

I have given you all this history for a reason. My father committed suicide.

On a sunny spring morning of May 1994, my father went to work as usual, called my sister to wish her happy birthday, then went home around lunchtime. He removed all the items from his pockets save his driver's license, wrote final letters to all of us, took a small handgun from the closet, and drove to a remote area and shot himself in the head. You cannot imagine what I have felt concerning his death. Even now, two years later, I still cry at the thought of him, alone, in the car at the last moment. I see his face, clenched in pain, tears falling from his reddened eyes as he says, "I'm sorry," and pulls the trigger. Of course I did not see it, but in my mind that is how it happened.

I wish you could have known him. He was an inspiration to me. I also wish he could have known the two of you. He would have loved you more than anything, I am certain. He would most decidedly have spoiled you rotten!

The point I am trying to make in relating all this to you is this: Love.

Love yourself. Love your family. Love your life. Love everything and everyone you can and never resist the opportunity to tell them. I told my father about my love for him in a letter I wrote to him the Father's Day before his death, and that act, that small token of love, a simple letter, has been my only salvation, my only peace in my father's death. Sophia, Camille, be honest about your feelings. If someone hurts you, say so. If someone pleases you, say so. If you love someone, tell them. Life is so short and death is forever.

I LOVE YOU,

I LOVE YOU,

I LOVE YOU,

MAMA

DEAREST DAUGHTER,

*Y*ou are 20 months old and you formed your first sentence today: "I want banana." As time goes on you will form more sentences, and sooner or later one of those sentences will be, "Do I have a daddy?" I want you to know that even before you were born I started thinking about how to answer that question.

When you are four I will hold you close to my heart and tell you about all of the people in your life who love you dearly. I will also tell you that I love you and will take care of you forever.

When you are seven or eight I will tell you that I have never met your daddy and that a doctor helped me get pregnant by taking your daddy's seed and planting it in my body. I will tell you that many children, including children with a mommy and a daddy, those with two mommies or two daddies, and children with one mommy or one daddy, are born that way. I will also tell you that I love you and will take care of you forever.

THIS SINGLE PARENT WRITES TO HER DAUGHTER WHO WAS CONCEIVED THROUGH DONOR INSEMINATION.

When you are 13 or 14 I will tell you that when you were born your daddy lived in Oakland, California, and worked in a hospital as a patient-service representative. I will tell you that if you want, we can try to find out more about him when you are a little older. I will also tell you that I love you and will take care of you forever.

When you are 18 I will tell you that you, and only you, can contact the fertility clinic and obtain the name and other identifying information about your donor at any time. I will tell you that the donor doesn't know your name but that he was notified when you were born that his sperm donation resulted in a birth. I will tell you that other children were born to women inseminated with his sperm but that I don't know any of the other mothers and don't know if any attempts have been made to contact him.

I won't have to tell you that your blond hair and blue eyes come from him, but I will tell you that he, like you, likes bagels and yogurt.

I will tell you that the decision whether to contact him is yours.

I pray that the choice I made about your conception was a good one. I believe with all my heart that it was.

I LOVE YOU, MY DAUGHTER, AND WILL TAKE CARE OF YOU FOREVER,

MOM

DEAR ERIN,

I know that you have had to deal with a different lifestyle than a lot of other children. Yes, you not only have divorced parents (unfortunately, that's not the different part), but you also have parents who are both in the air force and always, it seems, stationed just as far apart as possible. I miss you every time you visit Dad and I know he misses you when you're here. Just remember, every time we move or each time you go on a visit, home is not a house or a place. Home is when you're with people who love you. Erin, you are loved so much by so many.

Still, I know it's been hard on you sometimes, and once you told

me you would never join the military. Well, like Grandma told me while I was growing up and her mother told her, I will support you and be your biggest fan in whatever you choose to do, whether it be the president of the United States or a fan dancer.

I want to let you know why I joined the service and have made a career of it these last 15 years. I spent nine years in military intelligence and the last six years in recruiting. I have always felt I was making a major contribution to our country, but when I came into recruiting and worked in communities, I found that some people don't appreciate the work, dedication, or sacrifice I or my military family have given.

KAREN HAS A FULL-TIME CAREER IN THE UNITED STATES AIR FORCE AND WANTS HER DAUGHTER TO UNDERSTAND THE DEDICATION SHE FEELS IN PRESERVING THE U.S. CONSTITUTION.

Once a man approached me while I was in uniform and told me just how mis-
guided I was for being in the military. I listened and didn't say much except that he
had the freedom to say anything he wished. When he left, someone else who had over-
heard him asked me how I could listen to all of that and not get angry. My answer was
simply, How could I? I took an oath to support and defend the Constitution, which
allowed him that very form of freedom he was exercising—the freedom of speech.
I would give my last breath to protect that freedom and all the other freedoms outlined
in that document so that you, all my loved ones, and the rest of this nation can continue to exercise them.

Many of our family have taken that same oath, and I'm proud to follow in their
footsteps, but I am just as proud of the rest of our family who choose different paths:
teaching, medicine, law, engineering, business, and so on. Whatever you choose to do,
just do it to the very best of your ability, and no matter what, I am and will always be
so very proud of you.

I LOVE YOU CLEAR UP TO THE SKY,

MOM

DEAR MARIAH, BEVERLEY, AND DIEDRE,

When I first came to America, I felt lost and very upset about being taken away from everything and everyone I had known since birth. My parents moved me, at the age of 19, from Hong Kong to America. There were many changes in the way we had to live, and it was a very traumatic time in my life. At that time, I made a promise to myself that I would not do anything like that to my children. So, when your father and I decided to take you to Oregon, I told him that we had to do it while you were still young enough to adjust easily. Once again, I left all I held dear to me behind, in search of something better, but this time it was my duty to search for a better life for my children.

I have always told all of you that you can do anything you put your mind to and that Mom and Dad will give you all the support, love, advice, and help you need to reach your goal. I have no doubts in my mind that each of you can be an astronaut, an Olympic athlete, or the first female president if that is what you want to do. Reach for the stars! My girls, you all have the ability in you to accomplish great things. Your dad and I will always be there to help out along the way. Sometimes it may seem as if we are being hard on you, pushing you to do things that are too hard, but in the end you will come to understand that sometimes a little push is not a bad thing; in fact, sometimes it is what is necessary.

SABRINA, WHO WAS SEPARATED FROM HER CULTURE, HERITAGE, AND ALL THAT WAS FAMILIAR, NOW UNDERSTANDS THOSE DIFFICULT CHOICES THAT MUST BE MADE IN THE BEST INTEREST OF HER CHILDREN.

The three of you carry within you the best of this world. You are a mixture of your father's culture and mine, but most of all you are you. I hope that we have taught you how important it is to know your heritage: my upbringing in a Chinese culture where your grandfather is the patriarch and your grandmother rules the home; also, your father's upbringing as an American, free to do and think as an individual who is important in his own right. As Americans, you are free to choose what to do with your lives and how you want to live it. We have always instilled in you the importance of individuality and how you must choose what you feel is right for you and not just what everyone else is doing.

Mariah, you are reaching that time in your life when these lessons will be very important. As you go into middle school, high school, and college, peer pressure will be something that you'll have to face. We hope that you will always feel comfortable in coming to either one of us with any problem you may have or just to talk. Sometimes

when you are a teen, that is all one needs, a good ear or a shoulder to cry on.

Beverley, you are the one that I worry about because you seem to let your heart rule you. You have learned how to put up a tough exterior, but I know beneath it beats a very tender heart. I hope that you will come to understand that what your dad and I have been trying to teach you all these years is to use your head and not always your heart. Sometimes, the heart knows when it must be stronger, but do not leave yourself wide open to get hurt.

Diedre, I have no doubts in my mind that if there is to be a female president in my lifetime, you will be right in the thick of it. Please do not lose any of the enthusiasm and zeal you have for life.

Finally, I would like to express how grateful I am that I had the opportunity to put down in words to the three of you how very proud and happy I am to be your mother. I would not change any one of you for anything in the world. You all have your faults, but who does not? A perfect child would be so dull, and life with you is not dull. I hope that each of you will have the opportunity to feel the immense love I feel each and every time I look at my three beautiful girls who will always be my babies.

LOVE ALWAYS,

YOUR MOM

MY DEAREST HANNAH,

*T*rying to untangle the myriad of complex feelings and emotions that I hold for you into words is way beyond my somewhat feeble literary abilities. However, I want to try to relate some thoughts and memories that I hold deep within me every day.

MARY SHEPHARD
PHYSICIAN
1928–1989

These are the words on the gravestone of my mother (always Mummy to me), your grandmother. She died from cancer the day after her 61st birthday, two and a half years before you were born. Mummy now lies in a picture-book English country village graveyard. Nearly all my childhood and adolescent life was spent in that village. My memories of her are intertwined with those of growing up there. She was full of energy and enthusiasm, and even during those testing teenage years I was always proud that my friends enjoyed her company and spending time at our house. It was Mummy who built us a tree house, fed our pet lambs at 3 A.M., cycled around the village lanes with us while we rode small unruly ponies, and slid down hillsides in the Lake District on her bottom with me. Not only was she a unique parent but a special person to her friends and within the community. A doctor who worked in the local schools, village halls, and health centers, she was much loved and respected. The Buckingham Cottage Hospital honored her by naming a new child development building after her.

HELEN REMEMBERS THE PLEASURES OF HER CHILDHOOD SPENT WITH A LOVING MOTHER WHOM HER DAUGHTER WILL NEVER KNOW.

I miss her immensely. I am only now truly appreciating her love of gardening and her talent for its design. But now it's too late to glean knowledge from her, and I blunder around the flower beds trying to remember the names of plants which evoke memories of my mother and my childhood, the ones I grow just because she did.

She would have been a wonderful grandmother and would have truly loved the socks off you! I can almost hear the giggles and shrieks that would have occurred. I am sad that you were never to know each other. However, having you in my life is an immeasurable joy. You are only four years old, but already you have grown from that frail, infection-laden baby placed back in the hospital at two weeks old to a strong and beautiful nymph-like child. Many facets of your personality remind me of Mummy, of our togetherness and fun. Watching you learning to ride a horse, your love of animals, your enthusiasm for life, and your ability to make a joke out of almost any situation evoke memories of Mummy, sometimes of a particular time past, other times just a general feeling.

You are such a special person in your own right, Hannah. You are bright, charming, and vivacious, and you have the potential of a great future. Growing up in England 35 years ago is so different from growing up now in America. I am looking forward to us learning about and experiencing it together. We both would have benefited from the wisdom and experience of your grandmother, had she been alive now. There are many times when I have wished that I could ask her advice. Raising a daughter is a challenge!

So, my little Hannah-Banana, as you grow up do not lose sight of your family: your daddy, brother Oliver, and me, who love you unconditionally. I hope that in the years to come you will be able to look back upon a childhood as happy as mine was, filled with love, fun, and security. I hope I will be here to share it with you for very many years to come and maybe slide down a few hillsides on our bottoms together!

You are a true treasure.

ALL MY LOVE,
YOUR MUMMY

DEAR KRISTI,

One thing that has been on my mind for some time is to explain to you in detail the history surrounding the reason I had breast implants and the resultant circumstances surrounding that decision, and how it has affected me, Dad, and, ultimately, you. The reason I feel I need to explain this to you is because of the journey on which it has brought me, what I have gained from it, and perhaps how it will benefit you.

As a young girl I had to deal with the belittling fact that I was unattractive and undesirable because I was very flat-chested. I wore falsies all of my life. I even felt I had to tell your father that I didn't have a bust before we were married (as if he couldn't tell) to make sure he still wanted me, knowing that fact. As far as that goes, about your dad's feelings, he has made it clear to me numerous times it didn't matter to him, it wasn't that important to him, and he has never made me doubt his word.

In 1985, a year after you, Jon, Dad, and I were hit by a drunk driver and my right foot was crushed in the impact, my self-esteem seemed to plummet. My foot was still very painful and needed surgery to correct it. When we saw the orthopedic surgeon, he described what he would do. Dad asked if it were possible to do more than one surgical procedure at a time. Dad and I had already discussed it, and he suggested

if my bustline really bothered me, maybe breast implants would help me feel better about myself. The doctor agreed and recommended a plastic surgeon, and the date was set. I remember when going into surgery I was not scared! I was excited because I knew the outcome would change my life for the better and I could feel whole.

No one outside a few friends and some family knew I had breast implants, not even you. No one needed to know, just me. I didn't need to flaunt it by wearing low-cut dresses or blouses (that just isn't me). But somehow it wasn't at all like wearing falsies; it was me now, inside, magic. My chin was up, not in haughtiness, but in the pride of being a real woman now, as man sees it.

Well, my life did change, at least my attitude did, as did my perception of myself. I went into business with a partner and loved it. I felt like I could do anything. But you know, for years my health seemed to deteriorate and I was easily fatigued. Then some media coverage of problems with the implants started to make sense, and many of the symptoms my doctors noted seemed to fit.

I decided to have the implants removed, and shortly before the surgery, Dad and I told you about it. I knew it was difficult for you to understand why I chose to have them in the first place. During that time I feared what I might look like afterward, fear of scarring and possibly no bust at all. But by then I had years to search my heart and find out that the person I really was, wasn't because I had larger breasts. Whatever I had was always there and I was able to let it out more freely because of the way I felt about myself. I was happy and content with my inner self and my physical looks. Losing my breasts, or the implants, wasn't going to take that away.

I want you to remember two things that I have learned. The first is that God has given each of us a package of problems or trials to deal with. With those problems you also have the innate ability and gifts to overcome them and excel. We must search our hearts and find the purpose for which they are intended.

Second, I learned you must always think well of yourself and realize your own worth. You are a pearl of great value. Don't ever forget those things, especially in your darkest moments. During my darkest moments I wasn't able to do a lot for you, but I hope you always knew I loved you. I know you love me. It all comes to light as we grow older, and I want to share that, with my hand in yours and a smile on my face.

May you be blessed with faith, courage, patience, and love throughout your life experiences. I will always be there for you.

TEENA TELLS HER DAUGHTER OF HER DECISION TO HAVE BREAST IMPLANTS AND OF THE SELF-ESTEEM AND HEALTH ISSUES SURROUNDING THAT CHOICE.

LOVE,

MOM

MY DEAREST SARAH AND KATIE,

*H*omework is done. The phone probably won't ring anymore tonight. You've gotten your things ready for school, brushed your teeth, fed the dog, fought over who gets the last cookie in their lunch tomorrow. I can feel the house breathe a sigh of relief as the lights go off one by one.

"I'm in!" That's my cue that you are ready for that sacred time that comes at the end of almost each day. I know that I look forward to it as much as you both do. I walk down the hall towards you and can hear the remnants of the last power struggle or the laughter that comes after one of Katie's weird jokes. There is always a place between you that has been saved for me. It's never okay that I lay on top of the covers. To get the full benefit of this experience we must be tangled together like hopeless shoelaces.

KRISTINE WRITES OF HER DESIRE TO PROTECT HER DAUGHTERS FROM THE PAIN AND DIFFICULTIES OF LIFE, ALTHOUGH SHE REALIZES THE IMPORTANCE OF SENDING THEM ON THEIR WAY AS INDEPENDENT AND CAPABLE YOUNG WOMEN.

We've read so many good books during these times before sleep. We've worked out a billion problems about boys, teachers, and friends. We've talked about sex and love and making the right choices. We've prayed, what seems like a million prayers, for loved ones, lost pets, sick friends, families in trouble. Sometimes we've laid in the dark and just listened to the sounds of the night.

After countless kisses and hugs you drift off to sleep. I finish the tasks that have quietly awaited their turn. Sometimes I'm too sleepy to get much more accomplished, but every night before I carry myself upstairs, I peek in on you both one last time.

I watch you sleep and I wonder about all there is to come to you in your lifetimes. It's hard to imagine that such gentleness will come up against the struggles we all must learn to battle. But in your very few years, you have already experienced your share of pain and suffering.

This last couple of years as we have watched your dad fight an immense battle with mental illness, he seemed to be disappearing right before our eyes. Suddenly it felt like life as we had known it was over. We have all had to deal with fear, confusion, and the impossible feeling of wanting to make everything okay. Yet, through it all you have never wavered in your support or commitment to your dad. As a result of very hard work on all of our parts, Dad is getting better.

There will be so many things that test your courage and convictions. There will be countless situations that call upon you to reach inside yourself and discover reservoirs of strength. I worry about you as women being faced with difficult choices that will shape your futures. There is a part of me that wants to stop the clock right now. I want to keep you safe and protect you. I want to tuck you in night after night.

But I know that I cannot protect you, just like my mother knew, and hers, and hers. What I must continue to do instead is to teach you, guide you, honor and respect you. You will make mistakes. What I hope for, though, is that you will learn from them and go on learning. I hope that you will make choices that shape you into the person you desire to become. Your foundation is a strong one, your sense of self seems clear. Trust that inner voice that you will come to know. And as I've said to you every night as I turn out your lights, "Remember who you are and what you stand for."

I'LL LOVE YOU ETERNALLY,
MOMMA

DEAR JENNY AND MARINA,

One of our greatest disappointments as a family was one miscarriage and three ectopic pregnancies. Your dad and I always wanted more than one child, and Jenny, you always wanted a sister.

We decided to pursue international adoption. We had observed open adoption in the United States in two different friends' lives. Both had to give up their new children to the birth parent, and it devastated them. But even beyond wanting to avoid the possibility of such a heartbreak, we felt strongly that the children in other countries needed homes so badly. After much research we chose Bulgaria.

Marina, you were one of six children born out of wedlock to your birth mom, whose only means of supporting herself was prostitution. Because of the law in that country, you had been offered to two Bulgarian families before we could have the chance to choose you. As we looked through the pictures that the orphanage provided, we came upon you, with your bright shining eyes and beautiful smile. Only after choosing you did we find out that your physical condition was an uncommon kidney reflux, the same condition that Jenny has. We knew that the two of you were meant to be sisters.

Our family began preparing for the flight to pick you up. Jenny, you were so excited. You helped pick out the clothes for your new sister to wear home. We had sent pictures of the three of us to the orphanage and had been told that you, Marina, would recognize and begin to bond with us at first sight. I wish they had told us the truth. You screamed in fright at the sight of us and clung to your caretaker.

This was not what I had dreamed of and imagined all these months of anticipation. Jenny, you were so frightened and confused. Yet I knew beyond a shadow of a doubt that God had brought Marina into our lives as the missing link. What I have come to realize is that we thought we were rescuing you. In your mind we were strangers who were kidnapping you from all that was secure and familiar.

The next few days were like a distant dream. You cried and screamed in terror and anger. You were grieving the loss of your life. Jenny, you cried in my arms night after night, wanting to take her back, sure that we must have made a mistake. We laid in bed and I cried along with you. I told you that it was hard for us, too, but your father and I knew that Marina was to be a part of our family. We couldn't raise her without your help.

It is now months later. The adjustments continue, but our bonds as a family grow daily. Marina, you light up when Jenny walks into the room. You follow her everywhere. Jenny, you wish your sister would give you a break, leave you alone, find someone else to follow—just like all big sisters feel. But you love her, too, and are beginning to make a place for her that only another sister can fill. I am so proud of you for your courage and willingness to do that.

I want you always to know that I can't imagine my life without either of you. You are precious beyond words. I have loved you both from the day you each came into my life. Jenny, you came through the womb; Marina you came from an orphanage. Each of you was placed in my life by God—He just brought you in through different doors.

I LOVE YOU, MY PRECIOUS DAUGHTERS,

MOMMY

JOAN TELLS THE STORY OF HER TRIP TO BULGARIA FOR MARINA AND OF THE ADJUSTMENTS REQUIRED WITH A CROSS-CULTURAL ADOPTION.

DEAR ANGELA, CARMEN, AND GINA,

J am writing this letter to express my thoughts, feelings, hopes, and desires for each of you. I love you, I thank God for you, and I am proud of the beautiful young women you have become, inside and out.

JOANNE SPEAKS TO THE IMPORTANCE OF UNITY AMONG PEOPLE OF DIFFERENT CULTURES AND THE CHALLENGES THAT OCCUR IN A MIXED MARRIAGE.

As African-Americans and as children of a racially mixed family, you have faced some difficult challenges in your lives. Although you have been blessed with a wonderful set of black relatives on my side and an equally wonderful set of white relatives on Dad's side—grandparents, uncles, aunts, and cousins—we live, unfortunately, in a racially divided society that does not always look favorably on the idea of "race mixing," resulting in a variety of responses and reactions to our unique family of black and white unity.

You have endured the stares of disbelief, the wagging heads of disapproval and open hostility, as well as the occasional warm smiles of acceptance and overt expressions of approval from kindred spirits. In every circumstance, however, you have always held your heads high and maintained your

dignity, letting the quality of your character radiate more visibly than the color of your skin.

You are like bridges of unity between the Dutch-Irish Catholic heritage of Dad's side of the family and the mix of predominantly African-American and Native American cultures on my side. It seems to me that you have a unique role to play in the world as ambassadors of peace, love, and unity between the races. Just by being who you are, you are naturally breaking down the walls of division in a racially divided nation and building bridges of hope between them.

My hopes for you are a God-centered, peaceful world of racial harmony, in which you can raise your children in an environment that is safe and free from all fear, distrust, and division—a world where love prevails and where the human race is the only one that really matters.

LOVE,

MOM

DEAR MARISA,

As I reflect upon my hopes and desires as you prepare for your upcoming marriage to Jon, foremost in my mind is your happiness. Your present happiness is evidenced by the sparkle in your eyes and the radiance of your being. Because of my desire for your continued happiness, I would like to share with you some of the important things I've learned from 25 years of loving and marriage. I believe these words of wisdom are some of the keys to a happy marriage.

To have a successful marriage takes a love that comes from the depth of your soul plus a persistent and resolute commitment to be patient, kind, and forgiving during difficult times. Life will bring challenges even without your invitation. You and Jon will need to rely upon your mutual love and inner strength to be your anchor in the storms of life.

Your relationship with Jon should take priority in your life. You should consider what's best for your continued friendship with Jon before family, friends, career, or children. There are numerous important relationships in your life that will be necessary for you to consider their priority when they seek to demand more of your attention. It is with mixed emotions that I tell you this. It is my ultimate joy for you to have found true love, but it is also the realization of my fear that you have grown up and life will never be the same for us again. There will be times when I will want you with me, but you will be with Jon. I apologize in advance for times that I might act hurt. I now better understand my own mother's hurt at times when I chose to be with your dad rather than her.

MARLA WRITES WORDS OF LOVE, HOPE, AND DREAMS FOR HER DAUGHTER'S FUTURE AS THEY PREPARE FOR HER DAUGHTER'S WEDDING.

Make your marriage the ultimate in equal partnerships, sharing in decisions and responsibilities equitably. Always find time for fun together. Life is stressful and you need regular doses of fun and relaxation. I consider fun and laughter to be the "glue" of a marriage. It can fix almost anything.

Give each other numerous daily doses of tender affection. Keep the romance alive by small acts of love and kindness. The love the two of you have has all the ingredients for a lifelong romance and courtship.

I could continue with my advice, but you will learn all I have learned and more. As your mother I love you as no other person can. I carried you in my womb and close to my heart while anxiously awaiting your birth. When I held you in my arms for the first time I knew you were special. Then when you took your first steps as a baby I was so

excited. Shortly after I felt a twinge of sadness when I realized these were your initial steps to independence from me.

I have loved being a part of each new step you have taken in your life. I have felt deep pride with each of your accomplishments since. This step toward marriage is significant. I am feeling great joy at the prospects of what lies ahead for you, and pardon me for the times I shed tears when I contemplate that my relationship with you is changed forever. You are an exceptional person, Marisa, and I'm so blessed to be your mother.

ALL MY LOVE FOREVER,

MOM

QUERIDA HIJA HERMILA,

I am writing you a letter to tell you a little about my experiences. As you know, when we lived in Mexico we lived in a small village. It was beautiful there, but we were also very poor. For that reason your father and I had to come to the United States. You were so small at that time, and it hurt me very much to be separated from you. We did not have another alternative. That is why, with all the pain in my heart, I had to leave you with my mother and come to this country.

Since that time I have had to work very hard so that I could make money to bring you here to live with me. It is so important to me that you and your brothers are able to have a good education. I did not have that opportunity, since my parents were also very poor. I want a better life for you.

ANDREA HAS WORKED IN THE UNITED STATES FOR II YEARS AND IS BRINGING HER CHILDREN TO THIS COUNTRY ONE BY ONE.

I want to tell you to stay strong and always try to come out ahead. You can do this without fear and with much faith in God. My own strength and faith have helped me in these last years that have been so difficult. For many reasons your father and I have had to go our separate ways. As hard as that was, I want you to know that I did not let that beat me down. On the contrary, I feel very proud that even with my struggles I have gained and continue to move ahead. I would like you to one day also feel proud of all that you are able to accomplish.

You know that life can be very difficult. Without a good education it is even harder. So I want you to always work hard and make the most out of your life. Don't be afraid, because I will always be with you whenever you need me.

Con todo mi amor,

Tu Mama

DEAR KALLYSTA,

Thirteen days before my 17th birthday I gave birth to you. A lot of people couldn't comprehend me, a teenage mother, being so thrilled about the birth of a child I hadn't planned for. It was as if I wasn't supposed to love you like another mother that is married and older. There were those who said I would never graduate,

never live the life of a normal teenager, and that emotionally, I wouldn't be able to handle the stress of motherhood. Those negative attitudes never really bothered me. From the moment I saw you I knew that we were meant to do great things in life, together. I love you as much as any mother could love her child.

Whether or not I would graduate was never a question in my mind. I had always done well in school. After you were born, I kept doing my work as usual, but now there was even more reason for graduating. It wasn't for me anymore, it was for you. I would do anything and everything to make sure that you had the best life possible. I strongly believe in the importance of a good education and that I must set strong examples for you. I want you to be the very best you can be, and I think that being the best I can be is the first step for you.

For a time I was unsure if I would be able to go to college. I had serious thoughts of giving up. Then I realized how important it would be for both of us. You were my motivation through everything. I must have done all right because I was accepted to a good college. I remember the day that I graduated from high school.

I felt like I had accomplished my first major step in our life together. You were the person that I wanted to share my joy with.

It's been said that when you have a child in your teens, your life as a teenager is essentially over. It is true I made a large jump to adulthood. I no longer did the things that I did before you were born. While my friends were at parties and doing other things young people do, I usually was hanging out with you. But I would rather be with you than out with a bunch of people that don't think the same way I do. I tried to get out there and socialize, but I always worried about getting home to you. Every time I go somewhere, I always think how I would rather be spending time with you.

Some people feel sorry for me and say that I don't get out enough. There is absolutely no reason to feel sorry for me! How can they feel sorry for someone that has such a precious gift? I am so blessed by your presence in my life. Never before had I known a love as true, unconditional, and innocent.

JENNIFER ILLUMINATES THE LIFE OF A TEENAGE MOTHER AND THE GOALS AND DREAMS SHE IS PURSUING FOR HER DAUGHTER AND HERSELF.

I don't think that my age ever made me more stressed out or more overwhelmed than any other first-time mother. I have always tried to do the best I can. I know that I have been a good mom to you. I am confident about my abilities as a mother, probably because you are the most important thing in my life. If I ever prided myself at doing something well, it is this.

You have had such an effect on my emotions, giving me a new range of them. I never thought I could love so much or hurt so badly for another person. It's impossible to tell you just how much you mean to me. But I hope that by telling you every day, and by being a good mother to you for the rest of my life, you will know how deeply I love you. You are my precious little girl. Never forget that, my Most Beautiful Angel.

LOVE,

MOM

Dear Jennifer,

I remember finding out I was pregnant with my first child at the age of 26. I was terrified yet thrilled at the prospect of becoming a mother, something I had always dreamed of. The pregnancy had the usual morning sickness but no major problems. The day I went to the hospital I didn't know I would have a beautiful daughter the next day—after 33 hours of labor and an emergency C-section. I was delighted to be the proud mother of you, an adorable little girl.

As the years passed I proceeded to cater to your every need. I allowed you to have everything your heart desired, which I realized too late was a big mistake. By the time you reached the fifth grade you were having a hard time dealing with the everyday problems of growing up. Each evening there were long talks and crying sessions late into the night. The next five years continued to be a difficult time for both of us. We tried some counseling, but it didn't seem to help a lot.

As we were getting ready for you to enter the 11th grade, I noticed you couldn't get enough sleep and would become ill after eating. I was beginning to suspect you might be pregnant, as you had been seeing a lot of your boyfriend that summer. We went to the store and purchased a home pregnancy test, and the results were positive. I didn't want to believe it could be true. We saw my doctor and she confirmed the worst: my little girl was going to have a baby.

FATIMA SHARES HER HEARTACHE AT LEARNING OF HER TEENAGER'S PREGNANCY AND THE HOPEFUL FUTURE SHE NOW SEES FOR HER DAUGHTER AND GRANDDAUGHTER.

I must have sat in the doctor's office and cried for an hour. As we left the office, I could not hide my broken heart and red, swollen face. You, on the other hand, were much calmer. We waited about a week before telling your father, but it was difficult to hide what we were going through. I knew your father would not take it well, and the day you told him he looked in total shock. He did not accept this unwanted news well at all. It was very difficult to be excited about his 16-year-old daughter beginning her junior year in school, pregnant, with no job or security besides her parents, who didn't want to be taking on this kind of responsibility. I didn't know if my marriage would survive this shocking blow. It definitely put us through the tests of a lifetime.

Somehow you managed to focus your energy on schoolwork and get on the honor roll. Some mornings you were so overwhelmed that you would begin crying and not be able to attend school. On those days I would encourage you to get ready, and we would spend the day together. We made it through the rough spots, one day at a time.

Near the end of your pregnancy I had this overwhelming feeling of respect and admiration for you and how you had dealt with all the adversity you were enduring on a daily basis. I remember surprising you with a bouquet of flowers and a card explaining how proud I was of you.

You managed to continue your schooling within a week of delivery, allowing you to finish the quarter. On April 10, 13 days before your 17th birthday, you woke me early and we went to the hospital. The baby's father and his family were there, and I was able to witness the birth of my granddaughter. I was the first family member that held her, and I instantly fell in love. She was so alert, staring at me with her big, dark eyes that followed the sounds across the room. And there you were, my daughter. You totally amazed me once again, handling yourself in a very grown-up way.

Kallysta is now 16 months old. I can't imagine life without her. She fills our days full of laughter and joy and has brought us all much closer together. Looking at your daughter every day reminds me that out of what seemed to be such a devastating situation came a true gift of joy. Most of all, Jennifer, you have turned into a very caring and loving mother. I must have done something right.

I see nothing but the brightest future for you, my precious. We have a long road to walk, but if we continue to help each other, we will reap the benefits of a fulfilling life.

LOVE YOU ALWAYS,

MOMMY

DEAR TAWNIE, THE DAUGHTER I NEVER HAD,

*Y*ou have three brothers now, all nearly grown. So much time has passed that I seldom think of you anymore. I guess Solzhenitsyn was right: we mortals are incapable of sustaining faithfulness or grief. Life goes on.

THIS MOTHER OF THREE BOYS WRITES TO THE DAUGHTER SHE MISCARRIED.

Yet, I loved you for the three months I carried you. I dreamed of the blue-eyed, blonde, chubby-cheeked girl you'd be. I planned to sew yards of pink ruffles and lace into your wardrobe. You had a family to welcome you. I hoped for giggling girlfriends for you, for a normal happy life, and for good health. Of course, it never came to be. The doctor had big long words for why I miscarried—again.

But this is an old sorrow, a quarter-century past. Now I remember and wonder. The boys are going their own ways— college, jobs, and they go so far, clear across the country. They feel their wings and want to fly, far away from Mom, it seems.

I wonder if a daughter would have been somehow different. Would you have stayed close, if not physically, at least kept in touch more?

I am sometimes jealous of my friends who are mothers of daughters. They seem to maintain a closeness and can share the misfortunes, whimsies, and giddiness of life. There are women in my family with whom I can share anything, and I guess always wanted to extend that to another generation, like a family heirloom.

I don't mean to carry on and make us sad. As I write I anticipate someday having daughters-in-law. It won't be the same as one I raised, but perhaps, Tawnie, in missing you, I will try harder to welcome them into the family.

WITH LOVE,

MOTHER

DEAR SUSIE,

I'm sure no mother ever forgets the first time she laid eyes on each of her children, and how much more so in your case! In my late 40s, the mother of three teenagers, I was nervous when I traveled to China to meet you. The only information I had about you was a faxed medical report with a picture of a moon-faced little girl who was described as "bowlegged." I knew that under Chinese law you needed to be classified as handicapped in order to be given to a family who already had children.

Imagine my relief when I was handed a rather small baby girl who simply looked me over quietly and then started to smile and play. Your foster mother came to say good-bye, and she looked just as cheery and playful as you. You had the straightest legs I had ever seen on a baby.

Susie, it was a long, sad, and yet hopeful story that led to your becoming our daughter. We are old enough to remember the dreams that moved people to support the Chinese Revolution, dreams of economic justice and equality, and to have seen firsthand how far this is from realization, not only in China, but on our planet as a whole. We remember the Chinese slogan, "Women Hold Up Half the Sky," and know only too well how girls may still suffer physical neglect or worse in China and throughout the world. But Susie, your people have never stopped looking for practical solutions to problems, so you and thousands of other little girls your age have been adopted by families all over the world. The Chinese government, in deciding to allow this to happen, had to place humanitarian concerns above national pride.

You have given us so much already! We are continually amazed and delighted by your brightness and your sweet, affectionate nature. I have been tremendously grateful, too, for the help I have received from family and friends in caring for you. In my middle age, I had grown complacent in my comfort, and my involvement in my personal goals had begun to narrow my circle of interaction and compassion. There is nothing like raising a baby to make a person feel, every day, like part of a mutual endeavor shared with all of humanity and to realize the miraculous effort of love that goes into the perpetuation of the human race.

Susie, our family lives in wonderful circumstances, and you will never go hungry or be without shelter. Please be grateful for such abundance, and in your own life do something to extend those circumstances to others. Your birth mother may not have had the resources to do that, but she took risks for you so that you may have life. Please pass her bravery on! Now you are living in a family and neighborhood that are culturally mixed, and with this complex heritage, we hope you will grow up to be broad-minded and compassionate, aware of the common humanity of all people. This will also be a gift you can pass on, for there is still a lot of prejudice in the world. Never give up your idealism, Susie! Your adopted mother will teach you to sing the words of an old Jewish saying: "All the world is a very narrow bridge, and the important thing is not to be afraid."

LOVE,

MOM

CAROL, A MOTHER OF GROWN CHILDREN, BEGINS MOTHERHOOD AGAIN IN MIDLIFE WHEN SHE ADOPTS A CHINESE BABY.

My loving daughter Noycita,

On this day I have so much to tell you that a hundred pages would not be enough to put my thoughts into words. I will be brief and touch on the most sensitive areas.

Above all, I give thanks to our God for all He has done in your life. He was your guide, the lamp at your feet, the one who never left you, and the one who answered when you called. Never lose trust in the Lord.

Noycita, when you were younger and our family was faced with trials, you would ask me how you could help. Your heart was so young to have felt such pain. But you were eager to help the family and to put your own pain aside. My daughter, I thank you for being so wise. When I gave you advice, you listened and put it into practice. You triumphed over all the tests that came your way, overcame them, and always smiled in the end.

LEONOR WRITES ON THE DAY OF HER DAUGHTER'S GRADUATION FROM COLLEGE.

I remember telling you the story of the seed, which I hoped you would never forget and would hold dear to your heart. God gave you an imaginary seed which can take many paths. Only you can control the path. The first is the path of The Forgotten Seed. Although each of us have the gift of the seed, not everyone will put it to use. Some will put the seed aside, planning to plant it some other day. But they never do; nothing ever becomes of the seed.

The next is the path of The Bush. You begin by providing all that the seed requires: light, water, and love—until one day you are confronted with trials and tests. The pressure of life begins to take a toll on you and you become satisfied with not reaching your goals and dreams. The seed is then left unattended and forgotten. Although the seed began to grow, its growth stopped and it only grew to become a bush.

The last is the path of The Tree of Many Branches. You nurtured the seed, gave it love, light, and water. Regardless of how hard life had become, you cared for the seed until it grew into a beautiful tree full of branches.

My daughter, it is up to you to choose the path. But remember: when you are old and gray and look back upon your life, which would you rather see? The Forgotten Seed, knowing that you wasted the chance that God gave you? The Bush, smiling because you had tried, but soon after frowning because you were not persistent in following your dreams? Or The Tree of Many Branches, with each branch representing a part of your life, the tribulations and trials, the triumphs and victories, each contributing to the full growth of your tree where your dreams have become a reality?

My darling, take this seed and make it a beautiful tree. Try to achieve each goal. For each branch that is a mistake, look back and learn from it.

Thank you for being the daughter that you are. I feel so full of joy this special day that I am able to forget all of my problems. This is a very wonderful day not only for you but for me as well. It signifies so much in my life. Thank you for bringing me such joy.

I LOVE YOU,

MOMMY

My girls,

During our recent family reunion I was called to give thanks for all my children. The house was pushed at the seams with you children and grandchildren. But as much activity as there was, the Lord was good again and blessed our time and brought us together.

You have all been taught to love the Lord our Savior. He has been the foundation of our family. He has been first place in our lives, and you have all learned how important He is. You were all raised to serve the Lord and to trust in Him for everything. He is so good and through Him all things are possible.

THERESSA TELLS OF HER THANKFULNESS FOR THE BLESSINGS AND JOY THAT ARE HERS BECAUSE OF HER FAMILY AND FOR THE FAITH THAT SAW THEM THROUGH THE HARD TIMES AS WELL AS THE GOOD.

I remember hearing so many times that we shouldn't have all you children. A house filled with 22 children was too many, according to some folks. They said we wouldn't be able to care for all of you. But your father and I worked hard to care for you, to make sure you were all educated and that you learned to find God inside yourselves. God has been faithful and we have been blessed, over and over again.

Our lives haven't always been easy. There were the house fires. The first one was bad, but we were all safe and went on to build a new, big house and chapel. But seven years later when the second fire took our home and everything we owned, I was devastated. I remember that I couldn't cry, I couldn't walk, I couldn't even pray. But somehow the Lord got us through that, all safe. Now we got another home and chapel. Even when you can't always ask for help, the Almighty is there with you. Have faith in God, and He will bear your burdens.

I always told you to be ambitious, to work hard where God put you, and you would find your gifts. Sometimes I'm afraid I made you workaholics. But the more you work, the better you feel about yourself and about life. Remember I always said, "Don't lay down too late in the bed. Get up early, when the air is blowing and the morning is cool, and give the Lord the first fruits of your lips."

I told you not to be grudgeful of something somebody else has but to be thankful for the blessings God gave you. I see all of you today with your own gifts and talents. You are teaching your children that loving the Lord is what life is all about and that the more you know God and serve Him, the more you know nothing is impossible to do.

I taught you all to be people, people. God is love! We are to love one another. That love makes a tie that binds us together and is undying. Care for one another, ask yourself if you were that somebody how would you want to be treated.

I am proud of my children. You are each as unique as the very days you were born on. Each one of you is individual and special. I always told you to love yourself, not to put yourself better than somebody else, but love yourself so you can do whatever you want.

When I was young I didn't get much of an education. I didn't finish the eighth grade. I got married. All the rest of 'em got an education, but I told myself that through God's help I could be whatever I wanted. No woman could beat me at anything if I worked hard where God put me. So I worked hard to care for my children and tend my home. This was my one opportunity and I was going to be the best at it that I could.

Remember that God is our life. You are His temple and He lives in you. Take care of yourself; love yourself as the Lord loves you.

Delight yourself in the Lord;
And He will give you the desires of your heart.
Commit your way to the Lord,
Trust also in Him and He will do it.

— Psalm 37:4–5

I LOVE YOU,

MOM

DEAR JAIME,

*A*s I write this letter to you, you've just graduated from high school. Normally, this is a milestone in life when a mother reflects back on all that she has taught or hoped to impart on her daughter and prepares to give advice for the future. But, then, our lives have been anything but normal, huh, sweetie? For us I think it's the opposite; instead, it's how much you have taught me in 18 years.

My first thought of you is of overwhelming, overflowing love. An unconditional love, born out of your being my firstborn, my vulnerable, disabled daughter. Being our firstborn we did not immediately recognize problems with your development. But it was a gradual process of acceptance, of letting go of dreams, goals, expectations, and learning to trust God for your future. You taught me that, Jaime.

You taught me about perseverance and how to be an advocate. There were so many new challenges in the medical field as well as the educational field. I was your voice. I learned to get people to see you as a person, not so very different from others, with needs and feelings and not just a sum of multiple handicaps.

You taught me how to be assertive yet to get along with others in the process. You taught me patience, a very hard lesson that I'm still learning—waiting on test results, waiting for any small sign of progress from hours, days, and years of working on skills in school and therapy. You taught me the value of what is really important in life. It wasn't my preconceived ideas of an orderly, successful, "happy" family, perfect as I could make it. But instead I learned the value of investing in lives, something that matters for eternity. I invested in you.

WENDY WRITES OF HER UNCONDITIONAL LOVE FOR HER EXCEPTIONAL CHILD, WHO HAS A RARE GENETIC METABOLIC DISEASE.

You have touched so many people's lives, just being you. People have developed more compassion and acceptance and tolerance by being a part of your life, especially me. Those who have taken the time to get to know you have come to love you, your social nature, your smile, your infectious laughter. They also cry for you when you are in pain, having your uncontrolled seizures, losing your eyesight. You have taught me joy for the little things and appreciation and thankfulness for things that are often expected or taken for granted. For many years you could not show love in return. What a joy and blessing it was to experience the first hug from you at age 5, or your first attempt at a kiss at age 16. I have learned to live with adversity and to find a measure of happiness in that. I have learned to face the pain of inadequacy, not being able to fix things for those I love.

The hardest part has come in learning to gradually let go of you. Having to put you in a foster home for the greater good of protecting medical and legal services for you as an adult was an agonizing decision, and continues to be. Our lives have been entwined daily. What an

empty spot there is when you are gone. Living with the knowledge that I will have to watch you degenerate and die is an almost unbearable prospect.

A mother always wants the best for her child. I have tried to give you that within my limited power, and I have prayed fervently for you. I have learned that health and happiness and giving of love are more important than all the rest.

If I could give you health and heal your disease, I would sacrifice all. But what I can do is give you unconditional love and wait patiently until we can walk and talk with you and do all the things mothers and daughters do together, in heaven one day. I am so thankful to have had the awesome responsibility and privilege to care for and raise you for 18 years. I would not have traded it for an easier path, for you have taught me what is most important in life.

You will always be my little sweetheart.

LOVE,

MOM

My story is this. In 1980 I felt that I should seek ordination in the Anglican Church. For the next 12 years I was involved in various ways in trying to encourage the church to ordain women. Today I am one of the first women to be ordained in the Brisbane Diocese.

I feel very strongly that my daughter and all women should have the opportunity and freedom to be who they are. I believe this is why we were created and this is what God desires for us—for our spouses, our sons, and our daughters. I know that there are still mountains to climb, that there are still changes to be made, but I know with absolute certainty that the costs are worth the reward—for myself, but most especially for those who follow. Therefore, I have addressed my letter to all my daughters, for my journey is one which has led me to want to empower and to liberate *all* women.

I hope that I would have found the time and the courage to talk with you even if there had never been a book. You and I have shared interesting times, and I hope that you have learned from my struggles as you have rejoiced in my successes. More than that, I hope that you and many others will gain from them.

For many women the world has been a hostile place. We have tried, usually unsuccessfully, to fit into a mold which was never going to fit. We have torn ourselves into tiny pieces trying to be "good wives" and "good mothers," "good cooks" and "good nurses," and, in recent times, "good employees." Very often we have failed, or if we have succeeded, it has been at great cost to ourselves. In trying to be what we were not, we lost who we were.

I believe that the world is changing, that you will not be burdened by guilt or indecision about careers and families, that your partners will understand about mutuality in relationships, that you will be "parents" rather than "mothers" and "fathers," that you and your friends will understand that being a woman means many things which are not exclusive to each other.

It has been such a joy to watch you grow up, to see you grow in confidence and become your own person, to see you and your friends step onto the threshold of a world which is slowly changing.

> MARIAN, ONE OF THE FIRST WOMEN TO BE ORDAINED IN AUSTRALIA AS AN ANGLICAN PRIEST, ADDRESSES THE EMPOWERMENT AND LIBERATION OF NOT JUST HER DAUGHTER BUT ALL WOMEN.

Ruth, my love, you know only too well my immense love for and pride in you. When I see before me a confident young woman and when others tell me what a beautiful daughter I have, I am proud, but it is not because I take any credit. I am proud and pleased for you because you are your own person. What you have and what you give to others comes from inside you, and whatever it is, it is very special and I know myself privileged to be your mother.

It is difficult for me to give you advice or to provide you with words of wisdom, for that would be to presume that I was wise or that I had discovered the answers. But if I have learned anything through my life or through my ministry, it is that God calls us to be fully ourselves, to be the person whom God created, and to be that person in every role. There is no such thing as a "wife" or "mother," there is only Ruth and Susan,

Marian and Kate, who remain Ruth and Susan, Marian and Kate whether they be wives or mothers or employees or managers. The most important goal in life is to find yourself and then to never lose it.

Ruth darling, I cannot live your life for you. You must make your own mistakes and learn your own lessons, but whatever you do and wherever you are, know that you are unique and that you are special. You have a great deal to give and you will be a blessing to many.

May you know yourself created in the image of God, who is life and love. May you face the world with confidence and joy, for who you are is who you are meant to be.

GOD BLESS YOU MY CHILD, MY DAUGHTER,

MOM

DEAR SUNMIET,

I look at your picture and see a true Indian princess. You have truly earned the eagle fluffs you wear and the eagle feathers you hold in your hand. I cannot begin to explain the pride I feel when I think that your father and I created you.

Growing up in our world is not easy, and doing it as successfully as you have is even more difficult. In many ways you have had to learn to live in two worlds, the world of your people and the reservation and the "white" world. Because of who you are this has not been easy. As a young girl going to school on the reserva-tion, you were very bright and in the talented and gifted program. Some of your fellow Indian students teased you for your commitment and abili-ties. Then, when you went to junior high off of the reservation, you were not readily accepted because you were an Indian. You never let this get in your way and have shown great strength and character by taking the stands you have, and all that you have accomplished.

In high school you became one of the few Indian students ever to hold a student-body office. Deciding to play soccer in your senior year, when there was no girls' team, you played on the boys' team and were awarded "most improved player" at the end of the season. I have told you it is okay to live in both worlds but that home is always where your people and roots are. No matter how long you are away, a part of you is always on the reservation. It makes me happy to know that when you marry you would like to return to the reservation to live and raise your children.

JEWELL CONFIRMS THE IMPORTANCE OF CELEBRATING ONE'S CULTURAL HERITAGE.

You are passionate about your cultural heritage. My family comes from the Lummi, Yakima, Haida, and Soowallie tribes, and your father from the Warm Springs, Wasco, and Umatilla tribes. You have said that you have so many tribes running through your blood that you could hold a one-woman

powwow! It pleases me that you want to know everything about each tribe in your line. We have taught you our cultural and traditional values, and you have lived by them even when it would have been easier to compromise. Today I hear your concern that even though many on the reservation continue the traditions of our people, the values and beliefs behind those traditions are being forgotten. The strength of our Indian people has always been in our traditional values: to always replace that which was taken from Mother Earth and to be thankful for everything, to be respectful to all people, and to live with integrity. The beliefs behind these traditions and values must be passed on if our people are to remain strong.

Sunmiet, your small frame and quiet spirit leads one to believe that you can be easily swayed, but what a shock when you feel it necessary to defend the things you believe in. You are gentle but strong, open and friendly, yet very much in command of your personal boundaries. Your gentle voice speaks clearly that which you believe.

You honor me by the young woman you have become, and it has been my honor to present you to the world. You will always be my baby girl, and I will always know what strength of character and what wonderful wit and intelligence you possess. Happy Birthday, Sissy.

YOUR LOVING MOM,
MOM

MY MOST PRECIOUS CHILDREN,

None of us knows what the future holds. It's been four years since I was diagnosed with AIDS. Now I think about the future a lot. Mostly what I think about is you kids. How you will manage without me, who will take care of you, what will your future be like, and what choices will you make without me around to be your mother?

The last four years have been so difficult in many ways. We are not in a stable financial situation since I am unable to work anymore. Without government assistance I don't know what we would do. I know that you are not comfortable accepting welfare and that there is a real stigma about this. But when I was working 12-hour days, I never had time with you and I got so tired that I really couldn't function at my job. I would rather be broke than not have had this time with you kids. I hope someday you'll understand.

There is so much you will have to understand. I am sorry that this disease has come into our lives. But the disease of AIDS is really not to blame. The disease of drug and alcohol abuse is

LOREA, WHO HAS AIDS, WRITES TO HER CHILDREN OF HER LOVE FOR THEM AND HER FEAR OF WHAT WILL HAPPEN TO THEM WHEN SHE IS GONE.

what got me into this situation. I started drinking at 13. It was a way to numb the pain that I felt all of the time. Alcohol robbed me of my parents, my dreams, everything. Then at such an early age it had control of me as well. Because of my addiction, I lost my ability to make good decisions for myself. I was searching for the parents that alcohol had taken away from me, and in my search I made bad choices in my relationships. I am afraid that you might make the same mistakes. Remember that alcohol abuse can lead to so many other abuses. But I never had any idea at the time that my life would be so affected and in turn affect you so much.

I've learned a lifetime of lessons this past four years. I've learned that denial and running from your pain doesn't work. AIDS is real and I have learned to live with it as best as I can. I have asked for help, something I was never very good at. I have learned to forgive myself as well as others. I spent so much of my life hating and angry. But I've come to learn that those feelings were really only destroying me.

I guess that I hated myself more than anyone else. I always felt that I was unworthy, somehow. It has only been through this process of dealing with AIDS that I have come to accept myself. I try to love each part, even the bad, because that is me. If there is any lesson I would want to leave with you, it is to love yourself. Find peace with who you are and don't look outside yourself for acceptance and love. Find it deep within yourself and treasure it always. When you love yourself like that, you will know the kind of love I will always have for you.

M O M

MY DAUGHTER, MY FRIEND,

*T*he memories we are constantly creating are so very significant in that they are what often sustains us when we are apart. No one can take our memories from us, and we can play over and over again whenever we want those that we choose. It is truly a wonderful part of our overall design.

I am writing you today about a memory that affected me and our relationship so deeply—and I've never talked to you about it. While it is not a pleasant memory in many ways, it is one that I want you to carry with you in life. At 15 years of age, you already have such an appreciation for the

PENNIE RECALLS THE DEATH OF A YOUNG GIRL AND THE AGONY SHE FEELS FOR THAT GIRL'S MOTHER.

value of life and such love for your friends and family. I just don't ever want you to let anyone or anything steal that quality from you.

You remember about four years ago you happily went off with what looked like more that one hundred other kids to a week-long church camp. I knew you'd have such a great time. You love seeing old friends and making lots of new ones. The day you were to come home I received a call to my office. One of the girls at camp had become sick and was taken by Life Flight to the hospital. I was told about the possibility of others being infected—something about everyone at camp having to be immunized before going home. Well, just enough information to alarm me somewhat. When I arrived to pick you up, the media was all there, all of the county health officials, and a lot of concerned parents. You kids all seemed fine. I learned a little about meningitis and the small likelihood that anyone else would be infected.

The horror unfolded over the next few days as we learned of this child's struggle to survive and the incomprehensible decisions her loving family was faced with. In what was a futile attempt to save her young life, first one leg was amputated, and soon after, the other, as her loved ones could only stand by—helpless and in disbelief and grief.

The church was full the day of her service. Young people everywhere, music, videos, and a pastor desperately seeking for words of comfort where there hardly could be any. My memory as I sat with you that day, however, is of the eyes of The Other Mother—the girl's mother. I saw in her eyes the excruciating grief that would be in the eyes and hearts of every loving mother anywhere on this great planet. What she had experienced that week was beyond anything most of us can comprehend.

I found myself, there with my arm around you, imagining what she would give to walk out of that room with her daughter. What would she give to drive her home just one more time? What would she give to hear her daughter once again bound through the back door and shout, "Mom, I'm home!"

I value and treasure each and every day we share on this earth, for I know that no matter how many we have, they will never be enough for us. You and I seem to have learned not to sweat the small stuff, for in the bigger scheme of things, it's all small stuff anyway. We usually save our few battles for the truly more important things in life. I have honored and loved you so very much from the moment I knew you were with me. What a blessing to have the daughter I would have handpicked had I been given the opportunity. God could not have blessed me more than He has with you and your brother, Jared. You two will always be the best work, the best contribution I will ever make. My most important work. I will always, no matter what, be in your corners. I love you so very much.

M O M

DEAR JENNIFER,

You have come a long way since the day you arrived in the world during an air raid on London in World War II. That was a very frightening time for all of England. You spent your first night, and every night after that for probably three months, in a bomb shelter that we shared with three other families. By the grace of God we not only survived but developed inner strength from the experience.

I stayed home with both you and your brother for one year. But then I needed to work. All the young men in England had been drafted into service, so the women worked. I was a police officer during those years. We were lucky to have had such good day nurseries established for our children. You played with other children and were able to eat some of your meals there, which allowed us to save more food rations for the weekends.

MARJORIE REMEMBERS RAISING HER STRONG-WILLED, INDEPENDENT DAUGHTER DURING WORLD WAR II AND DELIGHTS IN THE RELATIONSHIP THEY SHARE TODAY.

You were an adventurous child. At the age of two you wandered off while I was weeding the front lawn, and I found you hours later sitting on the counter at a liquor store! At three you wandered away while we were at the beach, and we found you sitting on the sand with a crowd of kids watching a Punch and Judy show. After that we had to put a rein on you since no playpen could hold you. At four you started kindergarten. Then in November 1947, three months before your fifth birthday, we immigrated to the United States.

Our family was sponsored by an aunt and uncle who had lived in Spokane, Washington, for quite some time. They had no other family around them and longed for young people for company and help with their chicken farm. I sold eggs and your dad went to work for Kaiser Aluminum, eventually working for himself selling real estate. It seemed that we settled in rather quickly.

You have always had a competitive, competent spirit. You were 12 when your dad was hospitalized after a heart attack. You baby-sat almost every night for a month just to help out. At 16 you started waitressing to buy your own clothes for college. You did this every summer vacation. After you got your horse, you never missed a horse show. You pursued your education and your career with the same conviction. You have gone on to impact the world with your knowledge, gifts, and talents.

Life hasn't always been easy for you and I. Like so many mothers and daughters, we had a time where our differences separated us. But I never doubted our relationship or the love we felt for one another. During those years we weren't close, I was involved

in volunteering in a crisis program. I gave the same advice to many mothers who were estranged from their daughters. I told them to be patient, to give their daughters time and space. That worked for us, and we are closer now than ever.

I am so proud of all you have accomplished. It pleases me to see you, in spite of your busy schedule, taking time to renew yourself with time in your beautiful garden and home. Gardening always gave me such pleasure, also. There is little I could add to your continued success, except to say this: "Hold on to love, hold on to happiness, sometimes elusive but obtainable and worth everything else."

ALWAYS,
YOUR LOVING MOM

AFTERWORD

READING MY MOTHER'S letter, I learn more about the bond between us. I am reminded, however gently, that this is the last person who has known me all my life and that when I lose her I lose a fundamental source of knowledge and comfort.

I did not know that I spent my first three months in a bomb shelter. I did know that my mother's character—that one draws inspiration and strength from adversity—is one of the great gifts she gave me.

I did not know that I was adventurous at such a young age. I did know that my mother was an even more adventurous child and adult but that an English upbringing forced her to restrain her natural curiosity. I often thought that the tensions between us when I was a young adult stemmed from her desire to protect me from censure while wanting to do all the things that she and a more permissive American society allowed me to do.

Mother always had a way of criticizing me, which I hated, while she provided more opportunities than she had had (horses, dancing, traveling) for escape. Only rarely did she compete with me in my races on horseback, but somehow I knew that she wanted to be the little girl free to gallop at breakneck speed.

The tension between us dissolved as I began to realize how much strength it took for her to chart an optimistic course through a hard life. The resentment at her resistance to the "soft" parts of parenting and friendship (hugs, compliments, acceptance, assurance) diminished as I learned to value the "hard" parts (persistence, endurance, character, optimism).

Would I be different if I had had a different mother? Would my mother have been different in another time and place? Probably, but it doesn't matter now. We respect and love each other.

As I read my mother's letter, I still wish for a little more "soft," but that feeling is brief. We are happy together in this time and place, which is, for us, as it should be.

—Jennifer James, Ph.D.

Jennifer James is the author of Women and the Blues *and other books.*

AN INVITATION
TO THE READER

FOR EVERY LETTER included in this book there were countless others just as valuable and inspiring. Without exception, every letter writer appreciated having a reason to write her letter. In the words of one mother, "I want to thank you for providing me the opportunity to put in words the love and commitment I feel for my daughter."

In truth, every mother has just such a letter to write. We invite you to write yours. If this seems to be an overwhelming task, here are some thoughts to help you.

What words of wisdom do you repeat over and over to your daughter?

If you could tell her one thing, what would it be?

What have you learned from her, and how has she inspired you?

What is painful in her life? What are her unique challenges?

What are your regrets in your relationship?

We found that the process of writing our own letters was as moving to us as it was to the women who shared their letters. We hope that these letters have inspired you and that you will also find value in the process of composing a letter to your own daughter or loved one. The following two pages are reserved for your letter and perhaps a favorite photo to transform this book into a family keepsake.

PHOTO CREDITS

LETTER	PHOTOGRAPHER	LETTER	PHOTOGRAPHER
Betty	Greg Sawyer	Karen	Ana Buthe
Matilda	Unknown	Sabrina	David Van Raden
Svetlana	Unknown	Helen	David Van Raden
Karla	David Van Raden	Teena	Tom Pierson
Julia	Carol Bernal	Kristine	David Van Raden
Laramie	Tom Pierson	Joan	Tom Pierson
Pamela	Molly Davis	JoAnne	Unknown
Ursula	Tom Pierson	Marla	Jill Marie Holscher
Sandra	Carol Bernal	Andrea	Kristine Van Raden
Eunice	David Van Raden	Jennifer	Kristine Van Raden
Lulin	Kristine Van Raden	Fatima	David Van Raden
Dan Dan	Unknown	Anonymous	Fred Van Raden
Amy	David Van Raden	Carol	Jill Marie Holscher
Geneva	Jill Marie Holscher	Leonor	Carol Bernal
Linda	David Van Raden	Theressa	David Van Raden
Molly	Jim and Cara Wilson	Wendy	David Van Raden
Anonymous	Fred Van Raden	Marian	Unknown
Janella	Carol Bernal	Jewell	David Van Raden
Susan	David Van Raden	Sunmiet	Unknown
Anonymous	Unknown	Lorea	Kristine Van Raden
Kathryn	Tom Pierson	Pennie	Tom Pierson
Dawn	Archna Shukla	Marjorie	Kristine Van Raden
Anonymous	Tom Pierson		